October 20 - 1960

To Mary

from Marj.

IN HIS NAME

IN HIS NAME

PRAYERS FOR THE CHURCH
AND THE WORLD

A Discipline of Intercession
based on Bible insights

prepared by

GEORGE APPLETON

EDINBURGH HOUSE PRESS
2, EATON GATE, LONDON, S.W.1
*   *   *
MACMILLAN AND CO. LIMITED
ST. MARTIN'S STREET, LONDON
1956

MACMILLAN AND COMPANY LIMITED
London Bombay Calcutta Madras Melbourne

THE MACMILLAN COMPANY OF CANADA LIMITED
Toronto

ST. MARTIN'S PRESS INC
New York

MADE AND PRINTED IN GREAT BRITAIN BY
THE GARDEN CITY PRESS LIMITED,
LETCHWORTH, HERTFORDSHIRE

More ready to hear
Than we to pray;
Giving without measure
More than we desire
or deserve;
Able to do exceeding abundantly
above all
that we ask or think—
to
CHRIST JESUS
be glory throughout all ages.

FOREWORD

For some years I have felt the need of a discipline of missionary intercession which would help me to pray for the work of the whole Church, and not just that of the Church to which I belong or the missionary society through which I take my share in the Church's mission. I also hoped for a scheme of prayer which would not present missionary intercession as a specialized and separate activity but something integrated in the full range of Christian faith and worship. When the Conference of the International Missionary Council held at Willingen in Germany during July 1952 expressed a need similar to my own, I felt encouraged to make some suggestions to the secretaries of the Council, who responded by asking me to try to meet our mutual need.

The secretaries of the British Council of Churches and my fellow secretaries in the Conference of British Missionary Societies were equally encouraging, expressing the need of some cycle of intercession to deepen the new covenant in Mission and Unity to which these two bodies have set their seal.

The result is this book of prayers and biddings, with the Scriptural insights which inspired them. It is not meant to rival or displace cycles of prayer used by Churches and missionary societies, but to be the wider and more general context in which their particular intercessions can be set.

When I speak of the Church, it includes for me all the Churches of Christendom, including the great Roman Catholic Church and the Ancient Churches of the East as well as the great reformed Churches of the West, and I have dared to pray only that the Church may be what Christ wills it to be.

Many friends have helped with this book of prayers for the World and the Church, and they will recognize the help that they have given, and share in any good effect that our joint effort may produce. Their hope and mine is that Christians in many lands may be awakened to pray with loving and persistent urgency for the world of men for whom Christ died, and for the Church which is the agent of His loving purpose.

G. A.

London, 1955

ACKNOWLEDGEMENTS

Thanks are due to the following publishers, copyright owners and authors for permission to use prayers (detailed on pp. 183-7) from the undermentioned sources:

British Broadcasting Corporation, *New Every Morning*. Messrs. Burns, Oates & Washbourne, Ltd., *The Life that is Light. Christian News-Letter*. Church of Scotland Prayer Union, *The Holy Tryst* (*1940-41*). Edinburgh House Press, *African Ideas of God*. The Epworth Press, *The Book of Offices*. Messrs. Harper Bros., *The World at One in Prayer*. Messrs. Longmans, Green & Co., Ltd., *Cambridge Bede Book; Meditations and Prayers; Per Christum Vinces; Prayers of Citizenship; The Splendour of God*. Messrs. A. R. Mowbray & Co., Ltd., *After the Third Collect; The Church in Germany in Prayer; The Prayer Manual*. Oxford University Press, *Book of Common Order of the Church of Scotland*, extracts used by permission of the Committee of Public Worship and Aids to Devotion; *Daily Prayer; A Diary of Private Prayer; The Kingdom, the Power and the Glory*. Society for Promoting Christian Knowledge, *Acts of Devotion; A Book of Prayers for Use in an Indian College; My God My Glory; A Procession of Passion Prayers; A War Primer*; and with The Holy Cross Press (U.S.A.), *With Christ in God*. Society for the Propagation of the Gospel, *Prayers of the World-Wide Church*. Student Christian Movement Press, Ltd., *A Devotional Diary; A Book of Prayers for Schools; Prayers in Time of War; Prayers New and Old*. Toc H Incorporated, *A Pocketful of Prayers; A Treasury of Prayers. United Church Observer* (Canada). Universities' Mission to Central Africa, *Prayers for Common Use*. World Dominion Press, *World Dominion, January 1934*. Church Missionary Society; Church Missions to Jews; Industrial Christian Fellowship; Oxford Mission to Calcutta; Society of St. John the Evangelist; the Bishop of Sheffield; the Executors of the late Canon Anson, and of Dean Armitage Robinson; the Rev. W. O. Fitch, S.S.J.E.; the Headmaster of

Uppingham School; Mrs. F. B. Macnutt; the Principal, Cuddesdon College; the Very Rev. E. Milner-White; the Rev. John R. G. Ragg; Mrs. William Temple.

The text of the *Book of Common Prayer* is Crown Copyright and the extracts from this are reproduced by permission. Some lines from the *Prayer Book as Proposed in 1928* have been printed with the permission of the Holders of the Copyright.

The extract quoted from the *Form and Order of Service of the Coronation of H.M. Queen Elizabeth II,* which is Crown Copyright, is reproduced by permission.

It will be noted that in the Scripture extracts which are set at the beginning of each section the Revised Standard Version (1952) of the Bible is used, unless otherwise stated. Gratitude is expressed to The National Council of the Churches of Christ in the United States of America and to Messrs. Thomas Nelson & Sons for permission to make use of these extracts, in which we have naturally retained the American spelling.

If the Compiler has inadvertently infringed any copyright, sincere apologies are offered; any omission will be rectified in future editions.

CONTENTS

WHEN YE PRAY

Our Father:
> God and Father of Jesus Christ,
>> whom we know only through thy Son;
>
> Father of all who have been made thy sons—
>> calling all men to be thy children;
>
> Our Father.

Which art in Heaven:
> Thou art from everlasting.
> In thee all things exist.
>> Highest and holiest,
>> eternal and perfect.
>
> To thee we lift our spirits
> who art in heaven.

Hallowed be thy Name:
> May all men know thee as thou art,
>> lifting their hearts to thee
>> in reverence and love.
>
> May every tongue confess thy Name,
>> for in no other name
>> will men find salvation.
>
> Hallowed be thy Name on earth as it is in heaven.

Thy Kingdom come:
> King in our hearts;
> Lord of our lives:
>> bringing every thought
>> into captive obedience.
>
> In our own country,
> in every country,
>> the laws of thy Kingdom
>> accepted and obeyed.
>
> Thy Kingdom come on earth, as it is in heaven.

Thy Will be done:
> Thy wise and loving will
> in which is our peace.
> Victory over evil,
> victory over self,
> the banishment of war.
> Men loving in brotherhood
>   as children of thine
>   serving each other.
> Thy will be done on earth as it is in heaven.

Give us this day our daily bread:
> Fill us with active pity
>   for the millions who hunger,
>   for the homeless and displaced
>   who live without hope,
>   for the sick and suffering
>   whom thou wouldest heal.
> Food too for the soul,
>   the Bread of Life
>   without which men faint,
>   hungering for thee.
> Give all this day their daily bread.

Forgive us our sins:
> Our open crying sins,
>   our secret, whispering sins
>   which thou alone dost know.
>   Our lack of love,
>   our falling short of thy glory;
> forgive, as we forgive.
> Forgive the selfishness
>   entwined with our nature;
>   the lack of care for others:
>   am I my brother's keeper?
>   Our failure to tell good news,
>   to bring men home to thee.

Teach us to hate the cruelty of men,
    all lust of power,
    all pride of race,
    all greed of gain,
    sin against the truth,
    resentment and revenge.
Forgive us our sins.

Help us to understand the need of others,
    the wrongs they suffer,
    their need of thy forgiveness.
Forgive them and us.

And lead us not into temptation:
    Let us not fall back into weakness and sin,
      nor grasp anything which is not thy will.
    Let us not rest content
      or helpless in face of need,
      cowardly in act or speech
      when called to witness
      that we belong to thee.

Deliver us from evil:
    Not overcome by evil
      but answering with good,
      with hope and courage high,
      founded in thee.
    More than conquerors
      through him that loved us.
    Enduring to the end
      as seeing thee, our Lord.

For thine is the Kingdom,
the power and the glory, for ever and ever.
So let it be. Amen, Amen.

I. THE GOD OF ALL

1. In the beginning God

In the beginning God created the heavens and the earth. . . .
Then God said,

> Let us make man in our image, after our likeness; and
> let them have dominion over the fish of the sea, and over
> the birds of the air, and over the cattle, and over all the
> earth, and over every creeping thing that creeps upon
> the earth. . . .

And God saw everything that he had made, and, behold, it
was very good.

Genesis 1: 1, 26, 31

Who has performed and done this, calling the generations
    from the beginning?
I, the Lord, the first, and with the last; I am He. . . .
Before me no god was formed, nor shall there be any
    after me.
I, I am the Lord, and besides me there is no savior.

Isaiah 41: 4; 43: 10, 11

I am the Alpha and the Omega,
    the beginning and the ending,
    says the Lord God,
who is and who was and who is to come, the Almighty.

Revelation 1: 8

4

Let us worship GOD the CREATOR,
praising him with the angels of heaven:

1.   WORTHY ART THOU, our Lord and our God,
      to receive the glory and the honour
        and the power:
    for thou didst create all things,
      and because of thy will
    they were, and were created.

praising him for his eternity:

2.   THOU, LORD, in the beginning
      hast laid the foundation of the earth,
      and the heavens are the works
        of thy hands:
    they shall perish; but thou continuest:
      and they all shall wax old
        as doth a garment;
    and as a mantle shalt thou roll them up,
      as a garment,
      and they shall be changed:
    but thou art the same,
    and thy years shall not fail.

praising him for his love of men:

3.   FOR THOU LOVEST all the things that are,
      and abhorrest nothing which thou hast made:
    for never wouldest thou have made any thing
      if thou hadst hated it.
    And how could anything have endured,
   if it had not been thy will?
  or been preserved, if not called by thee?
  But thou sparest all: for they are thine,
    O Lord, thou lover of souls.

Let us pray:

for all whose spiritual horizons are limited by space, matter and time;

for all who, in modern times, find faith in God difficult;

for our Buddhist fellowmen who do not believe in the existence of the eternal God;

for ourselves, lest our own shrunken ideas of God, or our failure to live as children of God, should hinder men from coming to him.

The Lord's Prayer

4. ALMIGHTY GOD, whose glory the heavens are telling,
   the earth thy power, and the sea thy might,
       and whose greatness
   all feeling and thinking creatures everywhere herald:
       To thee belongeth
   glory, honour, might, greatness and magnificence,
       now and for ever, to the ages of ages.

5. O ALMIGHTY GOD, without beginning and without end,
   the Lord of thine own works:
   We praise and bless thee that thou gavest
       a beginning to time,
       and to the world in time,
       and to mankind in the world;
   and we beseech thee so to dispose all men
       and all things
     that they may be gathered up in thee
       and thine endless heaven;
   through him who is the first and the last,
   thine everlasting Word, our Saviour Jesus Christ.

6. WORTHY OF PRAISE from every mouth,
       of confession from every tongue,
       of worship from every creature,
     is thy glorious Name, O Father, Son and Holy Ghost:
       who didst create the world in thy grace
       and by thy compassion didst save the world.

6

2. God with Men

In the beginning was the Word, and the Word was with
    God, and the Word was God. . . .
And the Word became flesh and dwelt among us, full of
    grace and truth; we have beheld his glory, glory as of
    the only Son from the Father. . . .
No one has ever seen God: the only Son, who is in the
    bosom of the Father, he has made him known.

S. John 1: 1, 14, 18

All this took place to fulfil what the Lord had spoken by
    the prophet:
Behold, a virgin shall conceive and bear a son, and his
    name shall be called Emmanuel (which means, God
    with us).

S. Matthew 1: 22, 23

Acts of Praise
7. BLESSED BE THE LORD GOD OF ISRAEL:
    for he hath visited and redeemed his people;
    and hath raised up a mighty salvation for us
      in the house of his servant David.

8. GLORY BE TO GOD on high,
    and in earth peace, good will towards men.
      We praise thee, we bless thee,
      we worship thee, we glorify thee,
    we give thanks to thee for thy great glory,
      O Lord God, heavenly King,
      God the Father Almighty.

7

9. HONOUR AND POWER ETERNAL be to thee, O God:
    King of kings and Lord of lords,
      who alone hast immortality,
      dwelling in light unapproachable,
    whom no man has seen, nor can see;
      and to thine only-begotten Son,
      who for us men and for our salvation
      came down from heaven, and was made man,
    and through his death and resurrection
      brought us life and immortality.

Let us pray

10. O GOD OUR FATHER,
    who didst ever receive the upright in heart
      to dwell with thee, as men with God;
      and of thy great love hast deigned,
        in Jesus Christ thy Son,
      to dwell as man with men:
    Make us worthy, we beseech thee,
      both to become thy guests,
      and to receive thee as ours;
    through the same Jesus Christ our Lord.

11. O FATHER, who hast declared thy love to men
    by the birth of the Holy Child at Bethlehem:
      Help us to welcome him with gladness
    and to make room for him in our common days;
    so that we may live at peace with one another
    and in goodwill with all thy family.

For our Hindu fellowmen, that they may
see in Christ the true Incarnation

12. LEAD them, O Christ, in thy love
    lead them from the unreal to the real
    lead them from darkness to light
    lead them from death to immortality.

13. ALMIGHTY GOD,
   who didst wonderfully create man in thine own image,
      and didst yet more wonderfully restore him:
   Grant, we beseech thee, that as thy Son
         our Lord Jesus Christ
      was made in the likeness of men,
      so we may be made partakers
         of the divine nature;
   through the same thy Son, Jesus Christ our Lord.

The Lord's Prayer

14. GOD, who didst show forth thy glory in Jesus Christ
         thy Son:
   Grant us so to live in him
         and he in us
   that our lives may reflect thy glory. *Amen.*

3. God in Men

Christ's promise of the Holy Spirit

> And I will pray the Father, and he will give you another
> Counselor, to be with you for ever, even the Spirit of
> truth, whom the world cannot receive, because it
> neither sees him nor knows him; you know him, for
> he dwells with you, and will be in you.
> I will not leave you desolate; I will come to you. . . .
> If a man loves me, he will keep my word, and my Father
> will love him, and we will come to him and make our
> home with him.

S. John 14: 16-18, 23

The coming of the Holy Spirit

> When the day of Pentecost had come,
> they were all together in one place.
> And suddenly a sound came from heaven
> like the rush of a mighty wind, and it filled all
> the house where they were sitting.
> And there appeared to them tongues as of fire,
> distributed and resting on each one of them.
> And they were all filled with the Holy Spirit.

Acts 2: 1-4

An ancient prophecy is fulfilled

> And it shall come to pass afterward, that I will
> pour out my spirit on all flesh;
> your sons and your daughters shall prophesy,
> your old men shall dream dreams,
> and your young men shall see visions.
> Even upon the menservants and maidservants
> in those days, I will pour out my spirit.

Joel 2: 28-29

15. To THEE, O CHRIST, O King exalted,
>> we offer up our due praise
>> and unfeigned hearty thanks
> for that thou hast sent down and dispersed abroad
>> thine own Holy Spirit
> to restore and renew the spirit of men,
> to be the first dedication of thy Catholic Church on earth
> and the first publishing of the gospel to all lands,
>> the bond of unity,
>> and giver of light and life;
>>> to whom with the Father and thee,
>>> one blessed Trinity,
> be ascribed all might, majesty, dominion, and praise,
>> now and for ever.

16. O GOD, THE HOLY GHOST,
> come to us, and among us:
>> come as the wind, and cleanse us;
>> come as the fire, and burn;
>> come as the dew, and refresh:
> convict, convert, and consecrate
>> many hearts and lives
>>> to our great good
>> and thy greater glory,
> and this we ask for Jesus Christ's sake.

17. O HOLY GHOST,
>> giver of light and life,
> impart to us thoughts higher than our own thoughts,
>>> and prayers better than our own prayers,
>>> and powers beyond our own powers,
>> that we may spend and be spent
>> in the ways of love and goodness,
>>> after the perfect image
> of our Lord and Saviour Jesus Christ.

18.   O GOD, we pray thee for our fellowmen
  who believe the world of nature
   to be indwelt by spirits,
  who see in the life of the spring
     and the tree
      and the fertility of the soil
  the action of spiritual beings.
 Grant that they may come to know thee
  as the Spirit of Holiness and Love,
 and be delivered from all fear,
  to worship thee
 with the love and reverence of sons,
  through Jesus Christ our Lord.

The Lord's Prayer

19.   Now the God of hope fill us
  with all joy and peace in believing,
  that we may abound in hope
  in the power of the Holy Spirit.   *Amen.*

4. God Himself

The unity of God
  Hear, O Israel: The Lord our God is one Lord,
    and you shall love the Lord your God with all your
      heart, and with all your
    soul, and with all your might.

Deuteronomy 6: 4-5

The three-fold Name
  Go therefore and make disciples of all nations,
    baptizing them in the name of the Father
      and of the Son and of the Holy Spirit,
    teaching them to observe
      all that I have commanded you;
    and lo, I am with you always,
      to the close of the age.

S. Matthew 28: 19-20

The three-fold Grace
  The grace of the Lord Jesus Christ
    and the love of God
    and the fellowship of the Holy Spirit
  be with you all.

II Corinthians 13: 14

Let us worship God for revealing the mystery of his Being
20. HOLY ART THOU, O GOD, the Father, who hast made
          of one blood
        all nations of the earth:
      Holy art thou, O God the Son, who hast redeemed
          all mankind
        from the power of darkness:

13

Holy art thou, O God the Holy Spirit, giver of life and
light,
by whom the whole Church is governed and
sanctified:
Holy art thou, O God the eternal and adorable Trinity,
for whose glory man and all created things are, and
were created:
Glory be to the Father, and to the Son, and to the
Holy Ghost:
as it was in the beginning, is now, and ever shall be,
world without end.

21. WE PRAISE THEE, O GOD,
we acknowledge thee to be the Lord.
All the earth doth worship thee,
the Father everlasting.
To thee all Angels cry aloud,
the Heavens, and all the Powers therein.
To thee Cherubim, and Seraphim
continually do cry,

Holy, Holy, Holy; Lord God of Sabaoth;
Heaven and earth are full of the Majesty of thy glory.

Let us pray

22. BLESS US, O GOD, Father, Son, and Holy Spirit,
with the vision of thy glory;
that we may know thee as the Father
who created us,
rejoice in thee as the Son who redeemed us,
and be strong in thee, the Holy Spirit,
who dost sanctify us;
keep us steadfast in this faith,
and bring us at the last
into thine eternal kingdom,
where thou art ever worshipped and glorified,
one God, world without end.

23. O God who art eternal and perfect,
     our minds reach upward to know thee.
   Grant us a true spirit of worship
        that gazes in wonder
     at the richness of thy personality and love.
   Help us to experience thee
     as Father, Son and Holy Spirit
   and to worship thee as one God—
     Creator, Saviour and Sanctifier,
   to whom be all glory and praise in earth and heaven,
     both now and to all eternity.

For our Moslem fellowmen

24. O Lord Jesus Christ, Eternal God,
     who didst send forth thy apostles
        in the three-fold Name
     to preach the gospel to every creature:
   We pray thee for Moslems in every land.
   We thank thee for their faithfulness
     to the divine unity and majesty,
   and we pray that by the wisdom of thy Spirit
   they may be brought to know
     the eternal relationship of love
        within the Godhead,
   and to see in thee the full and perfect Word of God,
        who livest and reignest
        in the unity of the Blessed Trinity,
     one God only, blessed for evermore.

The Lord's Prayer

25. Blessing and honour, and thanksgiving and praise,
        more than we can utter,
        more than we can conceive,
     be unto thee, O holy and glorious Trinity,
        Father, Son, and Holy Spirit,
     by all angels, all men, all creatures,
        for ever and ever. *Amen.*

5. *The God of History*

All nations, great and small, are destined to be God's people
> In that day there will be a highway from Egypt to
> Assyria, and the Assyrian will come into Egypt, and
> the Egyptian into Assyria, and the Egyptians will
> worship with the Assyrians. In that day Israel will be
> the third with Egypt and Assyria, a blessing in the
> midst of the earth, whom the Lord of hosts has blessed,
> saying,
> Blessed be Egypt my people, and Assyria the work
> of my hands, and Israel my heritage.

Isaiah 19: 23-25

All history before Christ was a preparation for his coming
> When the time had fully come, God sent forth his Son,
> born of woman, born under the law.

Galatians 4: 4

The divine plan, known in heaven, is being worked out on earth
> The kingdom of the world has become the kingdom of
> our Lord and of his Christ, and he shall reign for ever
> and ever. . . . King of kings and Lord of lords.

Revelation 11: 15; 19: 16

Let us praise God:
> for his activity in creation, in history, through Israel,
> supremely through the incarnation of Jesus Christ,
> and in the working of the Holy Spirit;
> for the revelation of God's purpose and righteousness in
> history;
> that he is fulfilling his design to bring all men into his
> family through Jesus Christ;
> that he is all-ruling, and that one day he will bring
> history to an end, and he himself shall be all in all.

16

26. O KING of men and master of our lives,
    entering into glory by thy cross,
    to whom all authority is given
    both in heaven and upon earth:
Come, Christ, enter into thy kingdom;
subdue the world by the power of thy love,
and be known and adored
    to all ends of the earth.

27. ALL THY WORKS praise thee, O Lord,
    and thy saints give thanks unto thee.
They show the glory of thy kingdom
    and talk of thy power;
    that thy power, thy glory,
    and mightiness of thy kingdom
        might be known unto men.
Thy kingdom is an everlasting kingdom
and thy dominion endureth throughout all ages.

28. THY KINGDOM COME,
    in the assurance to all nations of their right to life
        and freedom,
    in the deliverance of mankind from the slavery of
        armaments,
    in the establishment of the reign of law between
        nations,
    in the recognition of the rights of minorities,
    in the right use of the resources of the earth,
    in the rekindling of a passion for truth,
    in the opening of springs of mercy and compassion:
thy reign over every thought, affection and impulse
        of our being.

The Lord's Prayer

29. To HIM who sits upon the throne and to the Lamb,
    be blessing and honour and glory and might,
    for ever and ever. *Amen.*

6. The People of God

God's call to Abraham

Now the Lord said to Abram, Go from your country and your kindred and your father's house to the land that I will show you. And I will make of you a great nation, and I will bless you, and make your name great, so that you will be a blessing . . . and by you all the families of the earth will bless themselves.

Genesis 12 : 1, 2, 3

His covenant with Israel

And Moses went up to God, and the Lord called him
out of the mountain, saying,
Thus you shall say to the house of Jacob, and tell the
people of Israel: You have seen what I did to the
Egyptians, and how I bore you on eagles' wings and
brought you to myself. Now therefore, if you will
obey my voice and keep my covenant, you shall be
my own possession among all peoples; for all the earth
is mine, and you shall be to me a kingdom of priests
and a holy nation. . . .
So Moses came and called the elders of the people,
and set before them all these words which the Lord
had commanded him.
And all the people answered together and said,
All that the Lord has spoken we will do.

Exodus 19 : 3-8

Israel is to spread true religion over all the earth

And now the Lord says: It is too light a thing that you
should be my servant to raise up the tribes of Jacob
and to restore the preserved of Israel; I will give you
as a light to the nations, that my salvation may reach
to the end of the earth.

Isaiah 49 : 6

18

Their return to God will bring even greater benefits to the world
 Now if their trespass means riches for the world, and if
   their failure means riches for the Gentiles, how much
   more will their full inclusion mean! . . . For if their
   rejection means the reconciliation of the world, what
   will their acceptance mean but life from the dead?

Romans 11: 12, 15

Let us thank God:
 for his call of one man
   through whom all nations shall be blessed;
 for his call of one nation
   through whom all nations shall come to the truth;
 for the faithful few in Israel who remained true to
   the covenant and so prepared the way for Christ.

30. O LORD, who hast chosen to thyself a special people,
        Israel,
       through whom thy way might be known upon earth,
       thy saving health among all nations:
    Grant that we and all those who once were far off,
       but now have been made nigh by the blood of Christ,
         may with clearer eyes behold
       thy steadfast purpose for thy chosen people;
    and that they, seeing in Jesus their Messiah and
        Saviour,
       may with humility and penitence of heart
         seek thy forgiveness;
       through the same Jesus Christ our Lord.

31. O LORD, who didst send forth thine apostles everywhere
        preaching the word,
       look upon thine ancient people still scattered abroad:
       send to them the light of thy gospel,
         and hasten the time
       when thou, Lord Jesus, shalt become
       the glory of thy people Israel.

32.   O Lord, we beseech thee, let thy continual pity
           cleanse and defend thy Church;
        and, because it cannot continue in safety
           without thy succour,
        preserve it evermore by thy help and goodness;
           through Jesus Christ our Lord.

33.   O God, who didst choose for thyself a nation
           to be thy agent in the world
        and when it failed thee didst re-create it
           in the Church of thy Son:
        Grant that thy Church may be truly the Body of
           Christ,
             giving itself for the world
               as thou didst give thy Son
               and as he did give his life.
        Let thy Church be a light to the nations,
           the messenger of thy gospel,
           the agent of thy salvation.
        And to us who are members of thy Body,
        give faithfulness, obedience, zeal and love,
        that thy wise and loving purpose may be
           accomplished
        and all men may know thee as their God and
           Saviour,
             through Jesus Christ our Lord.

The Lord's Prayer

34.   Blessed be the Lord God, the God of Israel,
           who only doeth wondrous things:
        and blessed be his glorious name for ever;
        and let the whole earth be filled with his glory.
             Amen, and Amen.

7. The New Israel

So you see that it is men of faith who are the
    sons of Abraham. . . . So then, those who are men of
    faith are blessed with Abraham who had faith.

Galatians 3: 7, 9

So then you are no longer strangers and sojourners,
    but you are fellow citizens with the saints
        and members of the household of God,
            built upon the foundation
        of the apostles and prophets,
Christ Jesus himself being the chief cornerstone,
        in whom the whole structure
        is joined together
        and grows into a holy temple in the Lord,
in whom you also are built into it
for a dwelling place of God in the Spirit.

Ephesians 2: 19-22

But you are a chosen race,
        a royal priesthood,
        a holy nation,
        God's own people,
that you may declare the wonderful deeds
of him who called you out of darkness
        into his marvelous light.
Once you were no people
        but now you are God's people;
once you had not received mercy
        but now you have received mercy.

I Peter 2: 9, 10

Meditation
    Let us meditate on the Church Universal,
        the new Israel refounded by Christ,
            the community through whom God wills to bless
            and save all nations.

21

Let us remember how, inspired by the Holy Spirit,
  it spread out beyond the old Israel,
  proclaiming what God had done in Christ
  and calling men to accept his salvation.

Let us thank God for its faithfulness in facing persecution,
    for the Holy Spirit's protection in times of weakness
      and darkness,
    for the inner band who maintained the fires of faith
      and devotion when times were difficult.

Let us recall the medieval missionaries who brought the
      pagan tribes of the West to Christ,
    and the great missionary movement of the last 150 years,
    through which new Churches have been brought
      into being
    and are now taking their part in God's eternal
      purpose of blessing.

Let us pray

35.   O GOD, mighty to save, infinite in compassion towards
    the nations that know thee not, and the tongues
    which cannot speak thy name: We humbly thank
    thee that thou hast made the Church of thy dear
    Son the chariot of the gospel, to tell it out among
    the nations that thou art king, and to bear thy
    love unto the world's end; and for all thy servants
    who counted not their lives dear unto them on this
    employment, and for all peoples newly praising
    thee, we praise and bless thee, Father, Son and
    Holy Spirit, one Lord and God for ever and ever.

36.   O GOD, we pray thee for thy Church
      which is set today amid the perplexities
        of a changing order,
      and is face to face with a new task.
    Fill us all afresh with the Spirit of Pentecost.

Help us to proclaim boldly the coming of thy kingdom.
    And do thou hasten the time
when the knowledge of thyself shall fill the earth
    as the waters cover the sea.

37. BLESS all work in thy field: Bless thy messengers:
    Bless the seed of thy word
        and grant that it bring forth fruit.
    Bless all who are joined in thee:
    Bless thy Church.
Thou buildest thy kingdom amongst us;
Thou buildest thy kingdom in all the world.

38. ALMIGHTY AND EVERLASTING GOD, by whose Spirit
    the whole body of the Church is governed and
    sanctified: Receive our supplications and prayers,
    which we offer before thee for all estates of men in
    thy holy Church, that every member of the same,
    in his vocation and ministry, may truly and godly
    serve thee; through our Lord and Saviour Jesus
    Christ.

The Lord's Prayer

39. THOU ART WORTHY, O LORD, to receive power,
                and riches,
            and wisdom, and strength,
        and honour, and glory, and blessing.
For the light of thy everlasting gospel,
    sent forth to every nation, and kindred,
        and tongue, and people,
    shining so long amongst ourselves:
for thy Church, the pillar and ground of the truth,
    against which the gates of hell shall not prevail:
all glory be to thee, O Lord. *Amen.*

23

II. THE GOD-MAN

8. Jesus is Lord

The first confession

> Now when Jesus came into the district of Caesarea Philippi, he asked his disciples, Who do men say that the Son of man is?
>
> And they said, Some say John the Baptist, others say Elijah, and others Jeremiah or one of the prophets.
>
> He said to them, But who do you say that I am?
>
> Simon Peter replied, You are the Christ, the Son of the living God.

S. Matthew 16: 13-16

The Holy Spirit inspires each confession

> Therefore I want you to understand that no one speaking by the Spirit of God ever says Jesus be cursed!
>
> and no one can say Jesus is Lord except by the Holy Spirit.

1 Corinthians 12: 3

Every tongue shall confess

> Therefore God has highly exalted him and bestowed on him the name which is above every name,
>
> that at the name of Jesus every knee should bow, in heaven and on earth and under the earth,
>
> and every tongue confess that Jesus Christ is Lord, to the glory of God the Father.

Philippians 2: 9-11

Let us praise God:

> for the acknowledgement by men and women in all lands that Jesus is Lord;

24

for the faith of those in village and town who show by
their lives the lordship of Christ;

for those who venture forth into new lands to proclaim
Christ as Saviour and Lord;

for those who penetrate into new areas of thought and
work to claim them for the lordship of Christ;

for those who witness to Christ in places where Christians
are a small minority or where witness is costly,
dangerous or liable to be ridiculed;

for the communion of the faithful the world over who
worship and witness together in a non-Christian or
post-Christian environment.

The Lord's Prayer

40. WE BESEECH THEE, LORD JESUS, to enlighten thy
people, and always set their hearts aflame with the
fire of thy glory; that they may ever acknowledge
thee as their Saviour and inwardly behold thee as
their Lord, who with the Father and the Holy
Spirit livest and reignest, ever one God, world
without end.

41. O LORD, thou art the king of our spirits. Thou hast
issued orders to thy subjects to do a great work.
Thou hast commanded them to preach the gospel
to every creature. We are going on that errand
now. Let thy presence go with us to quicken us
and enable us to persevere in the great work until
we die. *By a Christian of the Hervey Islands*

42. O CHRIST OUR GOD, in our acts this day,
the words we speak, the thoughts we think,
the fulfilment of our common tasks,
the relationships of our ordinary life,
thy kingdom come, thy will be done,
on earth as it is in heaven.

THE GRACE of our Lord Jesus Christ be with us all. *Amen.*

9. Christ our Example

He opened the book where
        it was written,
The Spirit of the Lord is upon me, because he has anointed me to preach good news to the poor. He has sent me to proclaim release to the captives and recovering of sight to the blind, to set at liberty those who are oppressed, to proclaim the acceptable year of the Lord.
And he began to say to them, Today this scripture
has been fulfilled in your hearing.

S. Luke 4: 17-19, 21

Until we all attain to the unity of the faith and of the knowledge of the Son of God, to mature manhood, to the measure of the stature of the fullness of Christ.

Ephesians 4: 13

For to this you have been called, because Christ also suffered for you, leaving you an example, that you should follow in his steps. He committed no sin; no guile was found on his lips.

I Peter 2: 21-22

Meditation

43. LET HIM BE THY MODEL
        for thy every word and deed,
    moving or standing,
        seated, eating,
        silent or speaking,
        alone or with others.
        Study him
    and thou wilt grow in his love,
        in his company.
    Thou wilt gain sweetness and confidence
    and thou wilt be strengthened in every virtue.

Let this be thy wisdom
      this thy meditation
      this thy study
to have him always in mind
      to move thee to imitation
      to win thee to his love.

Let us pray

44.   O LORD JESUS CHRIST,
      who didst deign to be made like unto men:
            the sharer of our sorrows,
            the companion of our journeys,
            the light of our ignorance,
            the remedy of our infirmity:
      So fill us with thy Spirit
            and endue us with thy grace
      that as thou hast been made like unto us,
      we may grow more like unto thee,
            for thy tender mercies' sake.

45.   COME, LORD! come with me: see with my eyes:
      hear with my ears: think with my mind: love with
      my heart—in all the situations of my life.
      Work with my hands: my strength. Take, cleanse,
      possess, inhabit my will, my understanding, my
      love.
      Take me where you will, to do what you want, in
      your way.

The Lord's Prayer

46.   MAY THE LOVE of the Lord Jesus
            draw us to himself;
      May the power of the Lord Jesus
            strengthen us in his service;
      May the joy of the Lord Jesus
            fill our souls.   *Amen.*

27

10. *I am the Way*

You know the way where I am going.
Lord, we do not know where you are going;
   how can we know the way?
I am the way ... no one comes to the Father, but by me.
Lord, show us the Father, and we shall be satisfied.
Have I been with you so long, and yet you do not
   know me? He who has seen me has seen the Father.

S. John 14: 4-6; 8-9

If any man would come after me, let him deny
   himself and take up his cross and follow me.

S. Mark 8: 34

Act of Faith

47. LORD, I BELIEVE that thou art the way, the truth
and the life. Make me so to walk with thee that
by thee I may come to the Father; make my faith
strong to believe all that thou hast revealed, for
thou art the very truth. Give me thy life that I
may say, I live, yet not I, but Christ liveth in me.
By thy divine omnipotence direct and strengthen
my faith; by thy divine wisdom instruct and
enlighten it; by thy divine goodness sustain and
perfect it, that I may abide in thee, unchanging
to the end.

Let us pray

48. O ALMIGHTY GOD, whom truly to know is everlasting
life: Grant us perfectly to know thy Son Jesus Christ
to be the way, the truth, and the life; that ... we
may steadfastly walk in the way that leadeth to
eternal life; through the same thy Son Jesus Christ
our Lord.

49. Most loving Father, who willest us to give thanks
for all things, to dread nothing but the loss of thee,
and to cast all our care on thee who carest for us;
preserve us from faithless fears and worldly anxieties,
and grant that no clouds of this mortal life may
hide from us the light of that love which is immortal,
and which thou hast manifested unto us in thy
Son, Jesus Christ our Lord.

50. Our Father, we thank thee that thou hast raised us
from sleep. We are indebted to thy patience with us
when we fail to do thy will.
    It is known to thee that we are worthless.
    Thou seest our lack of love: forgive us.
    Fill us, our Father, with thy Holy Spirit
        that we may be able to love thee.
Thine outstretched hand is before us, extending gifts
to us. We have not held out ours to receive them.
Have mercy on us. Press open our hands and
deposit therein thy mercies.
Thou hast called us to gather, and we do but scatter.
Thou hast commanded us to follow thee,
        and we have not risen. Raise us, O God.
    Do not wait for what we shall do:
        go on, O Lord, with thy kindness.
    Make thy Name holy in this land
        through the mercy of our Lord Jesus Christ.

By a Nigerian Christian

The Lord's Prayer

51. Jesus, our Master, do thou meet us while we walk
in the way and long to reach the heavenly country;
so that, following thy light, we may keep the way
of righteousness, and never wander away into the
darkness of this world's night, while thou, who art
the way, the truth, and the light art shining within
us; for thy mercy's sake. *Amen.*

29

And the Word became flesh and dwelt among us, full of
     grace and truth;
  we have beheld his glory, glory as of the only Son
     from the Father.

S. John 1: 14

In many and various ways God spoke of old to our fathers
  by the prophets; but in these last days he has spoken to
  us by a Son, whom he appointed the heir of all things,
  through whom also he created the world.
He reflects the glory of God and bears the very stamp of his
  nature, upholding the universe by his word of power.

Hebrews 1: 1-3

Jesus spoke to them, saying,
  I am the light of the world; he who follows me will not
  walk in darkness, but will have the light of life.

S. John 8:12

And we know that the Son of God has come and has given
     us understanding, to know him who is true;
  and we are in him who is true, in his Son Jesus Christ.
This is the true God and eternal life.

I John 5: 20

Thanksgivings:
  for those of many races and nations who have been called
    out of the darkness of superstition and error, and out
    of the twilight of unredeemed religion, into the light
    of the truth of the Christian faith;

for the truthfulness and honesty that it demands of us,
the emptying from the heart of unworthiness of thought
and intention;

for the truth of the Bible to uphold and sustain and
guide us;

for the focusing of vision on the perfection of Jesus Christ,
true God and true Man;

for the release from bondage into the service of him
whose service is perfect freedom;

for the infection of the knowledge of the truth that comes
to us in those about us who have been with Jesus.

Let us pray

52. O LORD JESUS CHRIST,
who art the way, the truth, and the life;
we pray thee
suffer us not to stray from thee, who art the way,
nor to distrust thee who art the truth,
nor to rest in any other thing than thee,
who art the life.
Teach us by thy Holy Spirit
what to believe,
what to do,
and wherein to take our rest.
For thine own name's sake we ask it.

53. O GOD who art nigh to all them
that call upon thee in truth;
who art thyself the truth,
whom to know is perfect knowledge:
Instruct us with thy divine wisdom,
and teach us thy law;
that we may know the truth and walk in it;
through him in whom the truth was made manifest,
even Jesus Christ, thy Son, our Lord.

54. O THOU to whom we always look,
        lighten our hearts
        as the sun throws light
    upon the dark bushes around us.
May we always reflect thy radiance
    so that those who have not known thee
        may see thee in us.
In the name of the Great Light we ask this.

An African Christian teacher

The Lord's Prayer

55. ALMIGHTY GOD,
who hast sent the Spirit of truth unto us
        to guide us into all truth:
We beseech thee so to rule our lives
        by thy power,
    that we may be truthful
    in word and deed and thought.
O keep us, most merciful Saviour,
    with thy gracious protection,
that no fear or hope may ever make us false
        in act or speech.
Cast out from us whatsoever loveth or maketh a lie;
and bring us all into the perfect freedom
        of thy truth;
through Jesus Christ thy Son our Lord.

MAY ALL THE PEOPLES, from the rising of the sun,
    even unto the going down of the same,
cry aloud in thy praise with joyful voice,
        and say:
    Glory be to thee, O God,
    the Saviour of all,
        for ever and ever. *Amen.*

12. I am the Life

I came that they may have life, and have it abundantly. . . .
And this is eternal life, that they know thee the only true
God, and Jesus Christ whom thou hast sent.

S. John 10: 10; 17: 3

Whoever drinks of the water that I shall give him will
never thirst; the water that I shall give him will become
in him a spring of water welling up to eternal life.
He who believes in me, as the scripture has said, Out of
his heart shall flow rivers of living water.

S. John 4: 14; 7: 38

I am the resurrection and the life; he who believes in me,
though he die, yet shall he live, and whoever lives and
believes in me shall never die.

S. John 11: 25, 26

That which was from the beginning,
   which we have heard,
   which we have seen with our eyes,
   which we have looked upon
   and touched with our hands,
     concerning the word of life—
   the life was made manifest,
   and we saw it,
   and testify to it,
   and proclaim to you the eternal life
     which was with the Father
     and was made manifest to us—
that which we have seen and heard
   we proclaim also to you.

I John 1: 1-3

Meditation

In the knowledge of God through Christ,
  and our response to that revelation,
    is our eternal life.
All spiritual life comes from Christ.
He is the vitalizing energy of all that lives,
  the spring of whatever vitality we have.
As we commit ourselves in obedience to Christ,
  his life flows into us—
    abundant life,
  enough for our own deepest needs
  and running over for the use of others.
His life in us develops a new kind of life,
  which physical death cannot destroy.
If we do not let other people know
    of this unfailing source of life,
  we fail both in gratitude to Christ
  and in love towards our fellowmen.

Let us pray

56. ALMIGHTY GOD,
  who through thine only-begotten Son Jesus Christ
      hast overcome death,
  and opened unto us the gate of everlasting life:
We humbly beseech thee,
  that as by thy special grace preventing us
    thou dost put into our minds good desires,
  so by thy continual help
    we may bring the same to good effect;
  through Jesus Christ our Lord,
    who liveth and reigneth
    with thee and the Holy Ghost,
  ever one God, world without end.

57.   O LIVING GOD,
      in whom is the fountain of life:
    So teach us to know thee

through Jesus Christ
that we may share the power
of that eternal life
which is in him,
and that all our lives
may be brought into obedience
to thy holy will;
through the same Jesus Christ our Lord.

58.   O GOD, THE LIVING GOD,
who hast put thine own eternity
in our hearts,
and hast made us to hunger and thirst
after thee:
Satisfy, we pray thee, the instincts
which thou hast implanted in us,
that we may find thee in life,
and life in thee;
through Jesus Christ our Lord.

The Lord's Prayer

MAY THE LORD bless us,
and preserve us from all evil,
and bring us to eternal life. *Amen.*

13. *Not to destroy, but to fulfil*

Christ is the fulfilment
of Israel's hopes

> Think not that I have come to abolish the law
> and the prophets;
> I have come not to abolish them but to fulfil them.

S. Matthew 5 : 17

All spiritual light before Christ
came from him

> The true light that enlightens every man was coming
> into the world.

S. John 1 : 9

St Paul preaching before a
rural pagan congregation, says

> Men, why are you doing this? We also are men, of like
> nature with you, and bring you good news, that you
> should turn from these vain things to a living God who
> made the heaven and the earth and the sea and all
> that is in them. In past generations he allowed all
> the nations to walk in their own ways; yet he did not
> leave himself without witness, for he did good and
> gave you from heaven rains and fruitful seasons,
> satisfying your hearts with food and gladness.

Acts 14: 15-17

And at Athens he quotes
the witness of pagan writers

> In him we live and move and have our being;
> as even some of your poets have said,
> For we are indeed his offspring.

Acts 17: 28

Yet he is definite in his demand
for a new life for Gentile converts

You did not so learn Christ!—assuming that you have heard about him and were taught in him, as the truth is in Jesus.

Put off your old nature which belongs to your former manner of life and is corrupt through deceitful lusts, and be renewed in the spirit of your minds, and put on the new nature, created after the likeness of God in true righteousness and holiness.

Ephesians 4: 20-24

Salvation came through one nation,
that all nations should be blessed

For salvation is from the Jews.　　　　　*S. John 4: 22*

The Jews are entrusted with the oracles of God . . .

. . . and to them belong the sonship, the glory, the covenants, the giving of the law, the worship, and the promises; . . . and of their race, according to the flesh, is the Christ.

Romans 3: 2; 9: 4, 5

The Lord's Prayer

59.　　O GOD, who hast made of one blood
　　　　　　all nations of men
　　　　　for to dwell on the face of the earth,
　　and didst send thy blessed Son Jesus Christ
　　to preach peace to them that are afar off,
　　　　　　and to them that are nigh:
　　Grant that all the peoples of the world
　　may feel after thee and find thee;
　　　　　　and hasten, O Lord,
　　　　the fulfilment of thy promise
　　　　to pour out thy Spirit
　　　　　　upon all flesh;
　　　　　through Jesus Christ our Lord.

60. O ETERNAL WORD,
    who from the beginning hast revealed
    glimpses of truth and righteousness
    through prophets of many faiths,
      we praise thee
    that all that is of value
    is found fulfilled and perfected
        in thee,
    and all that is mistaken
    finds its correction
        in thee.
Do thou draw all seekers of truth and righteousness
        to thyself,
and vouchsafe to them the unsearchable riches
    that can be found in thee alone.
We rejoice in thy salvation, knowing
    that there is no other name
    by which men can be saved
    apart from thy blessed name,
      O Jesus Christ,
      our Saviour and our Lord.

MAY ALL THE NATIONS whom thou hast made
    come and worship thee, O Lord,
      and glorify thy name. *Amen.*

14. Behold, I make all things new

No one sews a piece of unshrunk cloth on an old
      garment; if he does, the patch tears away from it, the
      new from the old, and a worse tear is made.
And no one puts new wine into old wine-skins; if he does,
      the wine will burst the skins, and the wine is lost, and
      so are the skins; but new wine is for fresh skins.

S. Mark 2: 21-22

Therefore, if any one is in Christ,
      he is a new creation;
the old has passed away,
      behold, the new has come.

II Corinthians 5: 17

Then I saw a new heaven and a new earth;
    for the first heaven and the first earth
        had passed away, and the sea was no more . . .
and I heard a great voice from the throne saying,
    Behold, the dwelling of God is with men.
    He will dwell with them,
    and they shall be his people,
    and God himself will be with them; . . .
And he who sat upon the throne said,
    Behold, I make all things new.

Revelation 21: 1, 3, 5

Meditation
    Christ demands that if we belong to him,
    the whole of our nature must be re-made.
      It is not sufficient to deal with one or two sins
      or to add one or two new duties.
    We must be born again.

Respectable lives,
which avoid scandalous sins
and practise what men may judge generous giving,
    are not enough.
Christ demands conversion,
    the total offering of our souls and bodies,
    all that we are and all that we have.

Only then can Christ use us
    to make the new world which is his will.
Only then shall we understand
    how constantly he is making all things new,
    re-creating them in the original pattern
        which God willed for them.

Let us pray

61.   O GOD, who sitting on the throne sayest,
            Behold, I make all things new:
        Fulfil now thy work in thy Church.
            Instil into it a sense
                of the brotherhood of nations.
            Form them into one great family.
        Let every nation with new devotion
            bring its peculiar gifts,
            and lay them at thy feet,
            to be adornments of thy kingdom;
                that we may see fulfilled
                the saying that is written,
        The kingdom of the world is become
        the kingdom of our Lord and of his Christ.

62.   O JESUS CHRIST, who art the same yesterday, today
        and forever: Pour thy spirit upon the Church that
        it may preach thee anew to each succeeding
        generation. Grant that it may interpret the
        eternal gospel in terms relevant to the life of each

new age, and as the fulfilment of the highest hopes and the deepest needs of every nation; so that at all times and in all places men may see in thee their Lord and Saviour.

63.   I AM no longer my own, but Thine.
     Put me to what thou wilt,
      rank me with whom thou wilt;
    put me to doing, put me to suffering;
let me be employed for thee, or laid aside for thee,
    exalted for thee, or brought low for thee;
    let me be full, let me be empty;
    let me have all things, let me have nothing;
I freely and heartily yield all things
    to thy pleasure and disposal.
And now, O glorious and blessed God,
    Father, Son and Holy Spirit,
    thou art mine, and I am thine. So be it.
And the covenant which I have made on earth,
    let it be ratified in heaven.

The Lord's Prayer

MAY THE LORD forgive what we have been;
    sanctify what we are;
   and order what we shall be;
    for his Name's sake.   *Amen.*

III. THE SAVIOUR OF ALL

15. Come unto Me

Hearken to me, O house of Jacob, all the remnant of the
house of Israel, who have been borne by me from your
birth, carried from the womb;
even to your old age I am He, and to gray hairs I will
carry you. I have made, and I will bear; I will carry
and will save. *Isaiah 46: 3, 4*

Come to me, all who labor and are heavy-laden, and I will
give you rest.
Take my yoke upon you, and learn from me; for I am gentle
and lowly in heart, and you will find rest for your souls.
For my yoke is easy, and my burden is light.

S. Matthew 11: 28-30

Apart from me you can do nothing. *S. John 15: 5*

Let us pray:
that men everywhere may hear and receive these
promises of a gracious and loving saviour;
that they may lay at his feet their burdens of sin, sorrow,
difficulty, and worry, and may find their rest in him;
that the Church may preach this gospel with courage and
love, knowing that Christ alone can satisfy men's
deepest needs.

64. O LORD, thou hast made us for thyself,
       and our hearts shall find no rest,
       until they find their rest in thee.

The Lord's Prayer

65. GRANT, we beseech thee, merciful Lord, to thy faithful
       people pardon and peace, that they may be cleansed
       from all their sins, and serve thee with a quiet mind;
       through Jesus Christ our Lord.

66. O LORD GOD, in whom we live, and move, and have
       our being, open our eyes that we may behold thy
       fatherly presence ever about us. Draw our hearts
       to thee with the power of thy love. Teach us to be
       anxious for nothing, and when we have done what
       thou hast given us to do, help us, O God our Saviour,
       to leave the issue to thy wisdom. Take from us all
       doubt and mistrust. Lift our thoughts up to thee in
       heaven, and make us to know that all things are
       possible to us through thy Son, our Redeemer.

67. LET US NOT SEEK OUT OF THEE what we can
                only find in thee, O Lord!
       Peace and rest and joy and bliss,
         which abide only in thine abiding joy.
       Lift up our souls above the weary round of
         harassing thoughts to thy eternal Presence.
       Lift up our minds to the pure, bright, serene
         atmosphere of thy Presence,
                that we may breathe freely,
                there repose in thy love,
                there be at rest from ourselves
                and from all things that weary us:
       and thence return, arrayed in thy peace,
                to do and to bear
                whatsoever shall best please thee.

GRACE to you and peace be multiplied in the
knowledge of God and of Jesus Christ our Lord.
                                             Amen.

43

16. The Gospel of Forgiveness

*Let us remember the many texts in the New Testament
which proclaim God's full and free forgiveness*

My son, your sins are forgiven. *S. Mark 2: 5*

Father forgive them; for they know not what they do.
S. Luke 23: 34

The saying is sure and worthy of full acceptance, that
Christ Jesus came into the world to save sinners. And
I am the foremost of sinners. *I Timothy 1: 15*

But God shows his love for us in that while we were yet
sinners Christ died for us. *Romans 5: 8*

God was in Christ reconciling the world to himself, not
counting their trespasses against them, and entrusting
to us the message of reconciliation. *II Corinthians 5: 19*

If any one does sin, we have an advocate with the
Father, Jesus Christ the righteous; and he is the expia-
tion for our sins, and not for ours only but also for the
sins of the whole world. *I John 2: 1, 2*

So we are ambassadors for Christ, God making his
appeal through us. We beseech you on behalf of
Christ, be reconciled to God. *II Corinthians 5: 20*

Let us thank God:
    for conscience operating in men everywhere,
        reminding them of their need of forgiveness;
    for God's free gift of forgiveness,
        which cannot be earned or won or deserved,
        but only accepted simply and trustingly;
    that God not only forgives,
        but gives us grace to conquer sin;
    that he has entrusted us with this good news
        that sin can be forgiven.

68. REJOICE over me, O God the Father, that this thy child was lost, but is found; was dead, but is alive again.

Rejoice over me, O God the Son, that thy loud cries and tears and bitter agonies which for my sake thou enduredst upon the cross, were not so unhappily lost, as to be cast away in vain upon me.

Rejoice over me, O God the Holy Ghost, that thy so many secret and powerful touches have at last got the upper hand of me.

Rejoice over me, O ye holy angels, whose ministry it is to rejoice at the conversion of a sinner.

69. O GOD, whose nature and property is ever to have mercy and to forgive, receive our humble petitions; and though we be tied and bound with the chain of our sins, yet let the pitifulness of thy great mercy loose us; for the honour of Jesus Christ, our mediator and advocate.

70. GIVE US, O LORD, a humble spirit, that we may never presume upon thy mercy, but live always as those who have been much forgiven. Make us tender and compassionate toward those who are overtaken by temptation, considering ourselves, how we have fallen in times past and may fall yet again. Make us watchful and sober-minded, looking ever unto thee for grace to stand upright, and to persevere unto the end; through thy Son Jesus Christ our Lord.

The Lord's Prayer

UNTO HIM that loved us, and washed us from our sins in his own blood, and hath made us kings and priests unto God, and his Father,
unto him be glory and dominion, for ever and ever.
Amen.

17. *The Cross of Christ*

And I, when I am lifted up from the earth, will draw all
    men to myself.

S. John 12: 32

For God so loved the world that he gave his only Son, that
    whoever believes in him should not perish but have
    eternal life.

For God sent the Son into the world, not to condemn the
    world, but that the world might be saved through him.

S. John 3: 16-17

Why, one will hardly die for a righteous man—though
    perhaps for a good man one will dare even to die.

But God shows his love for us in that while we were yet
    sinners Christ died for us.

Romans 5: 7-8

For I decided to know nothing among you except Jesus
    Christ and him crucified.

I Corinthians 2: 2

Meditation

    It is the Cross of Christ that draws men
        in every country and in every age,
            more than his teaching,
        more than his life of holiness,
        more than his miracles of power and love.
    The Cross declares God's love for men;
        God loves men as much as this.
    The Cross shows what men's sins do to God;
        sin causes all this pain to God.
The Cross of Christ was a thing which happened historically,
    on a particular day, for all men.
Only when its significance becomes personal to each man
    can we realize its deepest meaning
        and say with St Paul,
The Son of God, who loved me, and gave himself for me.

46

71.   BLESSED BE THY NAME, O JESU,
            Son of the most high God;
        blessed be the sorrow thou sufferedst
            when thy holy hands and feet were nailed
                    to the tree;
            and blessed thy love when,
                the fullness of pain accomplished,
        thou didst give thy soul into the hands
                    of the Father;
            so by thy Cross and precious Blood
            redeeming all the world,
            all longing souls departed
            and the numberless unborn;
        who now livest and reignest in the glory
                of the eternal Trinity
                for ever and ever.

72.   O LORD GOD, keep ever in our remembrance
        the life and death of our Saviour Jesus Christ.
            Make the thought of his love powerful
                to win us from evil.
        As he toiled and sorrowed and suffered for us,
                in fighting against sin,
        so may we endure constantly and labour diligently,
            as his soldiers and servants,
                looking ever unto him
                and counting it all joy
            to be partakers with him in his conflict,
                his Cross, and his victory;
        through the same Jesus Christ our Lord.

The Lord's Prayer

O SAVIOUR OF THE WORLD, who by thy Cross and
precious Blood hast redeemed us: Save us and help us,
we humbly beseech thee, O Lord. *Amen.*

18. The Risen Lord

Jesus Christ our Lord,
    designated Son of God in power
    according to the Spirit of holiness
    by his resurrection from the dead.

Romans 1 : 4

Blessed be the God and Father of our Lord Jesus Christ!
    By his great mercy we have been born anew
            to a living hope
    through the resurrection of Jesus Christ
           from the dead,
    and to an inheritance which is imperishable,
        undefiled, and unfading,
        kept in heaven for you,
    who by God's power are guarded through faith
    for a salvation ready to be revealed
           in the last time.

I Peter 1 : 3-5

But in fact Christ has been raised from the dead,
    the first fruits of those who have fallen asleep.
For as by a man came death, by a man has come also
    the resurrection of the dead.
For as in Adam all die, so also in Christ
    shall all be made alive.

I Corinthians 15 : 20-22

Easter Praise

73.   THOU ART RISEN, O LORD!
        Let the gospel trumpets speak,
          and the news as of holy fire,
             burning and flaming and inextinguishable,
            run to the ends of the earth.

Thou art risen, O Lord!
  Let all creation greet the good tidings
      with jubilant shout;
    for its redemption has come,
    the long night is past, the Saviour lives!
    and rides and reigns in triumph
      now and unto the ages of ages.

74. Thanks be unto thee, O Christ,
    because thou hast broken for us
      the bonds of sin
  and brought us into fellowship
    with the Father.
Thanks be unto thee, O Christ,
    because thou hast overcome death
      and opened to us
    the gates of eternal life.
Thanks be unto thee, O Christ,
    because where two or three are gathered together
      in thy Name
  there art thou in the midst of them.
Thanks be unto thee, O Christ,
    because thou ever livest
  to make intercession for us.
For these and all other benefits
  of thy mighty resurrection,
thanks be unto thee, O Christ.

Easter Prayers

75. O God, who by the glorious death and resurrection
    of thy Son Jesus Christ,
  hast brought life and immortality to light:
Grant us so to die daily unto sin
  that we may evermore live with thee
  in the joy of his resurrection;
through the same Jesus Christ our Lord,
  to whom be glory and dominion
    for ever and ever.

76.   GRANT UNTO US, O GOD, to trust thee
            not for ourselves alone
        but for those also whom we love
            and who are hid from us
            by the shadow of death;
        that, as we believe thy power to have raised
        our Lord Jesus Christ from the dead,
            so we may trust thy love
            to give eternal life
            to all who believe in him;
        through the same Jesus Christ our Lord.

The Lord's Prayer

77.   THE GOD OF PEACE,
            that brought again from the dead
                our Lord Jesus,
            that great shepherd of the sheep,
                through the blood of the
                everlasting covenant,
            make us perfect in every good work
                to do his will,
            working in us that which is
            well-pleasing in his sight;
                through Jesus Christ,
            to whom be glory for ever and ever.   *Amen.*

19. The King of Glory

Enthroned in glory

Worthy is the Lamb who was slain, to receive power and wealth and wisdom and might and honor and glory and blessing.

To him who sits upon the throne and to the Lamb be blessing and honor and glory and might for ever. . . .

Revelation 5: 12, 13

Ever praying for us

Since then we have a great high priest who has passed through the heavens, Jesus, the Son of God, let us hold fast our confession.

For we have not a high priest who is unable to sympathize with our weaknesses, but one who in every respect has been tempted as we are, yet without sinning.

Let us then with confidence draw near to the throne of grace, that we may receive mercy and find grace to help in time of need.

Hebrews 4: 14-16

Preparing a place for us

Let not your hearts be troubled; believe in God, believe also in me.

In my Father's house are many rooms; if it were not so, would I have told you that I go to prepare a place for you?

And when I go and prepare a place for you, I will come again and will take you to myself, that where I am you may be also.

S. John 14: 1-3

Meditation

    Our hearts can be full of joy and confidence
        because Christ reigns
      on the throne of the universe,
      adored by angels and saints.
From his throne he orders his kingdom
    and pours down on his people
        his Holy Spirit.
As he gave his life on the cross
      so now he offers
that once-for-all perfect, eternal sacrifice
        in heaven,
        for ever interceding
    for us who know and love him,
    and for all who have not yet
availed themselves of his saving love.

Acts of Worship

78.   THOU ART THE KING OF GLORY, O CHRIST,
    thou art the everlasting Son of the Father.
When thou tookest upon thee to deliver man
    thou didst not abhor the Virgin's womb.
When thou hadst overcome the sharpness of death
    thou didst open the kingdom of heaven
        to all believers.
Thou sittest at the right hand of God
    in the glory of the Father.

79.   THEREFORE WITH ANGELS AND ARCHANGELS,
    and with all the company of heaven,
we laud and magnify thy glorious Name;
    evermore praising thee, and saying,
        Holy, Holy, Holy,
        Lord God of hosts,
heaven and earth are full of thy glory.
Glory be to thee, O Lord most High.

80. O LORD, THE KING OF GLORY,
    who through the eternal doors didst ascend
        to thy Father's throne,
    and open the kingdom of heaven to all believers;
grant that, whilst thou dost reign in heaven,
we may not be bowed down to the things of earth,
    but that our hearts may be lifted up
    whither thou, our redemption, art gone before;
who with the Father and the Holy Ghost,
        livest and reignest,
ever one God, world without end.

81. O GLORIOUS CHRIST, who in thy ascension didst enter
        into thy kingdom:
Remember, we pray thee, the countless millions
    who have not heard of the redemption
        which thou hast won for them.
Grant that they may learn, through thy Church,
    of the new and living way
    which thou hast opened for them.
Let them draw near in fullness of faith,
    to enter with thee into the holy place
        of the Father's presence,
    and receive forgiveness and peace.
So may they worship,
    with the innumerable company of angels
    and with the spirits of just men made perfect,
Father, Son and Holy Spirit, one God,
        blessed for evermore.

The Lord's Prayer

82. UNTO HIM that sitteth on the throne,
        and unto the Lamb,
    be the blessing and the honour,
    and the glory, and the dominion,
        for ever and ever.   *Amen.*

53

Truly, truly, I say to you, unless one is born of water and
the Spirit, he cannot enter the kingdom of God.
That which is born of the flesh is flesh, and that which is
born of the Spirit is spirit.

S. John 3: 5-6

And Peter said to them,
Repent, and be baptized every one of you in the name of
Jesus Christ for the forgiveness of your sins; and you
shall receive the gift of the Holy Spirit. For the promise
is to you and to your children and to all that are far off,
every one whom the Lord our God calls to him.

Acts 2: 38-39

I am the vine, you are the branches.
He who abides in me, and I in him, he it is that bears
much fruit, for apart from me you can do nothing.
Abide in me, and I in you. As the branch cannot bear
fruit by itself, unless it abides in the vine, neither can
you, unless you abide in me.

S. John 15: 5, 4

Do you not know that all of us who have been baptized
into Christ Jesus were baptized into his death?
We were buried therefore with him by baptism into death,
so that as Christ was raised from the dead by the glory
of the Father, we too might walk in newness of life.

Romans 6: 3-4

Let us pray:
for all who are preparing for baptism,
that they may give themselves wholly to Christ,
that they may let Christ transform their lives;
for all catechists and teachers
who help to prepare new converts for baptism;

for all baptized in infancy,
 that parents, godparents and the Christian community
 in each place may help them to grow up in Christ,
 in steadfast fear and love;
for all whom Christ is calling,
 that they may have the courage to confess him before
 men.

The Lord's Prayer

Let us remember:
 the day when we ourselves were baptized
  and became members of Christ,
      children of God,
 and inheritors of the kingdom of heaven.

83. ALMIGHTY AND EVERLASTING GOD,
 we thank thee that thou hast received us
 into the fold of thy Church.
  Let thy Spirit be upon us
  and dwell in us forever.
 Keep us, we entreat thee,
 under thy fatherly care and protection;
  guide us and sanctify us
  both in body and soul.
 Enrich us abundantly with thy heavenly grace,
 and lead us to witness a good confession,
 and to persevere therein to the end,
  through Jesus Christ our Lord.

84. WE HUMBLY BESEECH THEE, O LORD,
 that we who have been made thy children
  by adoption and grace,
  being dead unto sin
  may live unto righteousness,

and being buried with Christ in his death
   may crucify the old man,
and utterly abolish the whole body of sin;
and that, as we are made partakers of the death
      of thy Son,
so we may also be partakers of his resurrection:
   through the same Jesus Christ our Lord.

85.   ALMIGHTY AND EVERLASTING GOD,
      whose beloved Son became man
         for us men and for our salvation,
      and gave commandment to his disciples
      that they should go and teach all nations,
      and baptize them in the name of the Father
      and of the Son and of the Holy Ghost:
   Give us grace to be obedient to his command,
   and grant that all men may have new birth in him,
   and, being delivered out of the power of darkness,
      may be received into the kingdom of thy love:
      through the same Jesus Christ our Lord.

86.   THE LORD JESUS CHRIST be near thee to defend thee,
      within thee to refresh thee, around thee to preserve
      thee, before thee to guide thee, behind thee to justify
      thee, above thee to bless thee; who liveth and
      reigneth with the Father and the Holy Spirit, God
      for evermore.   *Amen.*

21. Christ our Food

Jesus said to them,
> I am the bread of life; he who comes to me shall not hunger, and he who believes in me shall never thirst . . .
> I am the living bread which came down from heaven; if any one eats of this bread, he will live for ever; and the bread which I shall give for the life of the world is my flesh. . . . Truly, truly, I say to you,
> unless you eat the flesh of the Son of man and drink his blood you have no life in you; . . . He who eats my flesh and drinks my blood abides in me, and I in him.

S. John 6: 35, 51, 53, 56

For I [Paul] received from the Lord what I also delivered to you, that the Lord Jesus on the night when he was betrayed took bread, and when he had given thanks, he broke it, and said,
> This is my body which is for you. Do this in remembrance of me.

In the same way also the cup, after supper, saying,
> This cup is the new covenant in my blood. Do this, as often as you drink it, in remembrance of me.

For as often as you eat this bread and drink the cup, you proclaim the Lord's death until he comes.

I Corinthians 11: 23-26

Behold, I stand at the door and knock; if any one hears my voice and opens the door, I will come in to him and eat with him, and he with me.

Revelation 3: 20

Let us reflect how in the Holy Communion
>> the night of Christ's birth,
>> the night in which he was betrayed,
>> the hours upon the cross,
>> the morning of resurrection,
>> the glory of the ascension,
>> and our own worship and need
> are brought together in one eternal moment.

Let us thank God that throughout the world
>> the Holy Communion is the most loved and
>> solemn act of Christian worship;
> that in this Sacrament Christ comes to us in forgiveness
>> and love, to unite us to himself, to transform us
>> for his service.

Let us offer an act of deepest penitence that Christians of
different Churches are not yet able to meet together
in unity at the Lord's Table.

We come at Christ's command
87.   LORD, THIS IS THY FEAST,
>> prepared by thy longing,
>> spread at thy command,
>> attended at thine invitation,
>> blessed by thine own word,
>> distributed by thine own hand,
>> the undying memorial of thy sacrifice
>>> upon the cross,
>> the full gift of thine everlasting love,
>> and its perpetuation till time shall end.

> LORD, this is Bread of heaven, Bread of life,
>> that, whoso eateth, never shall hunger more.
>> And this the Cup of pardon, healing, gladness,
>>> strength,
>> that, whoso drinketh, thirsteth not again.
> So may we come, O Lord, to thy Table;
>> Lord Jesu, come to us.

We join in the worship of the Church all down the ages

88. IT IS VERILY meet and right, holy and becoming
         Lord God, Father Almighty,
     to worship thee, to hymn thee, to give thanks unto thee,
         to return thee praise both night and day,
     with unceasing mouth, and lips that keep not silence,
         and hearts that cannot be still.

We ask for sanctifying grace

89. STRENGTHEN, O LORD, the hands which have been
         stretched out to receive thy holy things, that they
         may daily bring forth fruit to thy divine glory.
     Grant that the ears which have heard thy songs may
             be closed to the voice of clamour and dispute;
         that the eyes which have seen thy great love may
             also uphold thy blessed hope;
         that the tongues which have uttered thy praise may
             speak the truth;
         that the feet which have walked in thy courts may
             walk in the region of light;
         that the souls and bodies which have fed upon thy
             living Body may be restored to newness of life.
     And with us may thy great love for ever abide,
         that we may abundantly render back praise,
         praise to thy Sovereignty.

90. AND HERE WE OFFER AND PRESENT UNTO THEE ourselves,
         our souls and bodies, to be a reasonable, holy, and
         living sacrifice; and we beseech thee mercifully to
         accept this our sacrifice of praise and thanksgiving,
         as, in fellowship with all the faithful in heaven and
         on earth, we pray thee to fulfil in us, and in all
         men, the purpose of thy redeeming love; through
         Jesus Christ our Lord, by whom, and with whom,
         in the unity of the Holy Spirit, all honour and
         glory be unto thee, O Father Almighty, world
         without end. *Amen.*

IV. MAKING MEN WHOLE

22. Lord, What is Man?

What is man, that thou art mindful of him, and the son of man that thou visitest him?

Bible answers—

91. A creature made by God
The image of God
A servant of God
A child of God
A sinner in need of forgiveness
The brother for whom Christ died

A member of Christ's Body
A friend of God
A fellow-worker with God
A temple of the Holy Spirit
A partaker of the divine nature
An heir of eternal life

92. O God, who hast prepared for them that love thee such good things as pass man's understanding: Pour into our hearts such love toward thee, that we, loving thee above all things, may obtain thy promises, which exceed all that we can desire; through Jesus Christ our Lord.

What shall I render unto the Lord for all his benefits toward me?

93. My reverence as a creature
My receptiveness to the divine impress
My duty as a servant

My love as a son
My penitence as a sinner
My gratitude as a brother redeemed
My joy in my fellow-members
My understanding as a friend
My co-operation as a fellow-worker
My welcome as his dwelling-place
My desire to be like him
My thankfulness as an heir
My life now and forever.

94. PRAISE THE LORD, O MY SOUL,
   and all that is within me praise his holy Name.
Praise the Lord, O my soul,
   and forget not all his benefits;
      Who forgiveth all thy sin
      and healeth all thine infirmities;
Who saveth thy life from destruction
and crowneth thee with mercy and loving-kindness.

95. BLESSED BE THE LORD GOD of Israel
   for he hath visited and redeemed his people . . .
   to give knowledge of salvation unto his people
      for the remission of their sins,
   through the tender mercy of our God
   whereby the day-spring from on high
            hath visited us,
   to give light to them that sit in darkness,
         and in the shadow of death,
   and to guide our feet into the way of peace.

96. ALMIGHTY GOD, who didst wonderfully create man
   in thine own image, and didst yet more wonderfully
   restore him: Grant, we beseech thee, that as thy
   Son, our Lord Jesus Christ was made in the likeness
   of men, so we may be made partakers of the divine
   nature; through the same thy Son, who with thee
   and the Holy Ghost liveth and reigneth, one God,
   world without end.   *Amen.*

23. *Wilt thou be made whole?*

I came that they may have life, and have it abundantly.

As he passed by, he saw a man blind from his birth.
And his disciples asked him, Rabbi, who sinned, this man
  or his parents, that he was born blind?
Jesus answered, It was not that this man sinned, or his
  parents, but that the works of God might be made
  manifest in him.

S. John 10: 10; 9: 1-3

And preach as you go, saying, The kingdom of heaven is
  at hand. Heal the sick, raise the dead, cleanse lepers,
  cast out demons. You received without pay, give without
  pay.

S. Matthew 10: 7-8

Let us thank God:
  that all down the ages the Church has followed her
    Master's example in caring for the sick and suffering;
  for the countless people who have found the God of love
    through the skill of a missionary doctor or nurse;
  for the selfless service of doctors, nurses, hospital workers,
    of many races, who show forth God's love in action;
  that through the revealing of the causes of disease and
    the secrets of health, disease is being mastered and men
    are finding the abundant life which God wills for them.

Let us pray:
  for all who suffer, that they may look up in faith to God
    to receive that strength which shall make them more
    than conquerors;
  that through the healing work of the Church men may
    be made whole in body, mind and spirit;
  for all Christian medical colleges, hospitals and dispen-
    saries and for all who work and train in them;
  that the Church in every land may teach men how to
    use suffering.

97. GRANT, O LORD, to all those who are bearing pain,
      thy spirit of healing,
        thy spirit of peace and hope,
        of courage and endurance.
   Cast out from them the spirit of anxiety and fear;
   grant them perfect confidence and trust in thee,
      that in thy light they may see light;
        through Jesus Christ our Lord.

98. MAY THE FATHER BLESS thee,
      who created all things in the beginning;
   may the SON of God heal thee;
   may the HOLY SPIRIT enlighten thee,
      guard thy body, save thy soul,
        direct thy thoughts,
   and bring thee safe to the heavenly country:
      who liveth and reigneth
        one God, world without end.

For doctors, nurses and health workers

99. O MERCIFUL FATHER, who hast made man's body to be
   a temple of thy Holy Spirit: Sanctify, we pray thee,
   all those whom thou hast called to study and
   practise the art of healing and the prevention of
   disease; strengthen them in body and soul, and bless
   their work, that they may themselves live as
   members and servants of Christ, and give comfort
   to those whom he lived and died to save; through
   the same Jesus Christ our Lord.

The Lord's Prayer

100. BLESSED BE GOD, even the Father of our Lord Jesus
   Christ, the Father of mercies, and the God of all
   comfort; who comforteth us in all our tribulation,
   that we may be able to comfort them which are
   in any trouble, by the comfort wherewith we
   ourselves are comforted of God. *Amen.*

24. With all thy mind

Hear, O Israel: The Lord our God, the Lord is one;
  and you shall love the Lord your God with all your heart,
  and with all your soul, and with all your mind, and with
  all your strength.

S. Mark 12: 29-30

Do not be conformed to this world but be transformed by
  the renewal of your mind, that you may prove what is
  the will of God, what is good and acceptable and perfect.

Romans 12: 2

Finally, brethren, whatever is true, whatever is honorable,
  whatever is just, whatever is pure, whatever is lovely,
  whatever is gracious, if there is any excellence, if there
  is anything worthy of praise, think about these things.

Philippians 4: 8

101. O God, who art the goal of all knowledge and the
      source of all truth, who dost lead mankind towards
      thyself along the paths of discovery and learning,
      direct with thy wise spirit the work of education in
      every land. Especially we would pray for those
      who have the difficult task of adapting new
      knowledge to the mind of ancient peoples. Give
      them insight into the needs of those whom they
      teach, humility to learn from their traditions, and
      wisdom to combine the old and the new. Above
      all, give them that grace and beauty of life without
      which all knowledge is vain.

Let us pray:
  that all Christian colleges and schools may be centres of
  Christian worship, learning and community

for a keen sense of vocation among all teachers
for the staff and students of training colleges in all lands
for closer co-operation between Church and home and
school in the work of education
for the guidance of the Holy Spirit in countries where the
Church has no direct share in education
for Christian teachers who work in State schools.

102. O THOU WHO ART THE GOD OF TRUTH AND LIGHT
as well as of love and righteousness: We pray for
the Christian schools and colleges of all countries,
that they may be such homes of fellowship and
brotherhood, learning and culture, that from them
shall come forth a stream of leaders to share these
blessings with their fellow-countrymen and to guide
their countries into the way of peace; through
Jesus Christ our Lord.

103. GRANT, O LORD, to all teachers and students,
to love that which is worth loving,
to know that which is worth knowing,
to praise that which pleaseth thee most,
to esteem that which is most precious unto thee,
and to dislike whatsoever is evil in thine eyes.
Grant us with true judgement to distinguish
things that differ,
and above all, to search out and to do
what is well-pleasing unto thee;
through Jesus Christ our Lord.

The Lord's Prayer

MAY THE PEACE OF GOD dwell in our hearts, and the
word of Christ abide in us richly in all wisdom. *Amen.*

25. *Give ye them to eat*

And when it grew late, his disciples came to him and said,
This is a lonely place, and the hour is now late; send
them away, to go into the country and villages round
about and buy themselves something to eat.
But he answered them,
You give them something to eat.

S. Mark 6: 35-37

What does it profit, my brethren, if a man says he has faith
but has not works? Can his faith save him?
If a brother or sister is ill-clad and in lack of daily food, and
one of you says to them, Go in peace, be warmed and
filled, without giving them the things needed for the
body, what does it profit?
So faith by itself, if it has no works, is dead.

James 2: 14-17

Come, O blessed of my Father, inherit the kingdom
prepared for you from the foundation of the world;
for I was hungry and you gave me food, I was thirsty
and you gave me drink, I was a stranger and you
welcomed me, I was naked and you clothed me, I was
sick and you visited me, I was in prison and you came
to me.
Lord, when did we see thee hungry and feed thee, or thirsty
and give thee drink?
As you did it to one of the least of these my brethren, you
did it to me.

S. Matthew 25: 34-37, 40

They shall hunger no more, neither thirst any more; the
sun shall not strike them, nor any scorching heat.
For the Lamb in the midst of the throne will be their
shepherd, and he will guide them to springs of living
water; and God will wipe away every tear from their eyes.

Revelation 7: 16, 17

Let us remember:
>   that three-fifths of the people of the world do not yet get
>   enough to eat;
>   that it is God's will that men should have all things
>   needful for full and happy life.

Let us thank God:
>   for his wonderful order of creation, for the germ of life
>   in the seed and for the bounty of harvest;
>   for the Food and Agriculture Organization of the United
>   Nations which is working with national governments
>   to increase food production;
>   for the growing number of agricultural missionaries who
>   teach men of many races that the earth belongs to God
>   and show them how to use it rightly.

Let us pray:
>   that nations may become true neighbours
>   that the Church may show men the example of caring
>   for one another
>   that the Christian community in every country may work
>   for social justice and mutual responsibility.

The Lord's Prayer

104. ALMIGHTY AND EVERLASTING GOD, who hast graciously
    given to us the fruits of the earth in their season,
    we yield thee humble and hearty thanks for these
    thy bounties, beseeching thee to give us grace
    rightly to use them to thy glory and the relief of
    those that need; through Jesus Christ our Lord.

105.   GIVE, O LORD, to all who till the ground
            wisdom to understand thy laws,
            and to co-operate with thy wise ordering
                    of the world:
       and grant that the bountiful fruits of the earth
            may not be hoarded by the selfish
            or squandered by the foolish,
       but that all who work may share abundantly
            in the harvest of the soil;
            through Jesus Christ our Lord.

106.   ALMIGHTY GOD, who fillest the earth with thy riches
            for the use of all thy children,
       have regard, we pray thee, to the impoverishment
                    of the nations;
            and on all who are in authority
            bestow thy gifts of wisdom and goodwill,
            that, being lifted above self-regard,
            they may establish a new order,
       wherein the needs of all men shall be supplied;
            through Jesus Christ our Lord.

107.   BLESSED BE THOU, O GOD,
            who bringest food out of the earth
            and makest the hearts of men glad
                    with thy goodness.
       Blessed be thou, for ever and ever.   *Amen.*

26. Peace on earth

Peace is God's gift to his people
> Let me hear what God the Lord will speak, for he will speak peace to his people, to his saints, to those who turn to him in their hearts.
> Surely his salvation is at hand for those who fear him, that glory may dwell in our land.
> Steadfast love and faithfulness will meet; righteousness and peace will kiss each other.

Psalm 85: 8-10

Peace is promised to all in Christ
> For to us a child is born, to us a son is given;
> and the government will be upon his shoulder, and his name will be called Wonderful, Counselor, Mighty God, Everlasting Father, Prince of Peace.
> Of the increase of his government and of peace there will be no end, upon the throne of David, and over his kingdom, to establish it, and to uphold it with justice and with righteousness from this time forth and for evermore.
> The zeal of the Lord of hosts will do this.

Isaiah 9: 6-7

Men fail to recognize where true peace lies
> And when he drew near and saw the city he wept over it, saying,
> > Would that even today you knew the things that make for peace! But now they are hid from your eyes.
> > For the days shall come upon you when your enemies will cast up a bank about you and surround you, and hem you in on every side, and dash you to the ground, you and your children within you, and they will not leave one stone upon another in you; because you did not know the time of your visitation.

S. Luke 19: 41-44

69

Let us pray:

that governments and peoples may continue to confer together and to look for ways of removing fear and suspicion;

for a determined effort to secure a higher standard of living in poorer and undeveloped countries;

that statesmen and leaders of public opinion may refrain from words and actions which stir up enmity and hatred;

that representatives of the Churches in countries between which tension exists may visit one another, gain a better understanding of one another and so promote reconciliation;

that Christians everywhere may unite in a common ministry of reconciliation in proclaiming Christ as the hope of the world;

for insight to recognize the seeds of strife in our own national prejudices and our self-righteousness;

that the nations of the world may understand and seek the things that belong unto peace—truth, justice, freedom, patience and goodwill.

For the leaders of the nations

108. ALMIGHTY GOD,
from whom all thoughts of truth and peace proceed:
Kindle, we pray thee, in the hearts of all men
the true love of peace,
and guide with thy pure and peaceable wisdom
those who take counsel for the nations of the earth;
that in tranquillity thy kingdom may go forward,
till the earth is filled with the knowledge of thy love;
through Jesus Christ our Lord.

109.   ALMIGHTY AND MERCIFUL GOD, without whom all
        things hasten to destruction and fall into nothingness:
        Look, we beseech thee, upon thy family of nations
        and men, to which thou hast committed power in
        trust for their mutual health and comfort. Save us
        and help us, O Lord, lest we abuse thy gift and make
        it our misery and ruin; draw all men unto thee in
        thy kingdom of righteousness and truth; uproot our
        enmities, heal our divisions, cast out our fears; and
        renew our faith in thine unchanging purpose of
        goodwill and peace on earth; for the love of Jesus
        Christ our Lord.

Finally, let us pray for ourselves

110.   LORD, make us instruments of thy peace.
            Where there is hatred, let us sow love;
            where there is injury, pardon;
            where there is discord, union;
            where there is doubt, faith;
            where there is despair, hope;
            where there is darkness, light;
            where there is sadness, joy;
        for thy mercy and for thy truth's sake.

The Lord's Prayer

111.   NOW THE GOD OF PEACE,
            that brought again from the dead our Lord Jesus,
                that great shepherd of the sheep,
            through the blood of the everlasting covenant,
        make us perfect in every good work to do his will,
                working in us
            that which is well-pleasing in his sight,
                through Jesus Christ;
            to whom be glory for ever and ever.   *Amen.*

71

27. Neither Jew nor Greek

The unity of mankind in Christ foretold
    I saw in the night visions,
        and behold, with the clouds of heaven
            there came one like a son of man,
        and he came to the Ancient of Days
            and was presented before him.
And to him was given dominion and glory and kingdom,
that all peoples, nations, and languages should serve him;
    his dominion is an everlasting dominion,
        which shall not pass away,
and his kingdom one that shall not be destroyed.

Daniel 7: 13, 14

The emnity between men abolished in Christ
        But now in Christ Jesus
you who once were far off have been brought near
        in the blood of Christ.
        For he is our peace,
        who has made us both one,
and has broken down the dividing wall of hostility,
    by abolishing in his flesh
    the law of commandments and ordinances,
that he might create in himself one new man
        in place of the two,
        so making peace,
    and might reconcile us both to God
    in one body through the cross,
    thereby bringing the hostility to an end.
And he came and preached peace to you who were far off
        and peace to those who were near;
    for through him we both have access
    in one Spirit to the Father.

Ephesians 2: 13-18

In Christ we are all born again,
so all distinctions are done away
> You have put on the new nature,
>> which is being renewed in knowledge
>> after the image of its creator.
> Here there cannot be Greek and Jew,
>> circumcised and uncircumcised,
>> barbarian, Scythian, slave, free man,
>>> but Christ is all, and in all.
> Put on then, as God's chosen ones,
>> holy and beloved,
>> compassion, kindness, lowliness,
>>> meekness, and patience.

Colossians 3: 10-12

Let us pray:
> that the mind of Christ
>>> may be in us
> to overcome all prejudice and self-consciousness
>>> of race or colour or tongue;
> for grace to bear no resentment
>>> when we or our fellow-countrymen
>>>> are criticized;
>>> for humility to examine ourselves
>>> to see if there is any truth
>>> in what is brought against us;
> for a readiness to open hearth and home
>>> to people of other races,
> especially to strangers visiting our country;
> for our brethren in countries where racial tension is acute,
>>> that they may work
>>>> with patience and understanding to abolish
> all forms of segregation and discrimination.

Let us thank God:
> for the new race of men which is created in Jesus Christ,
>> in which the power of the Holy Spirit overcomes
>>> racial pride and fear;

that within every nation there are
Christians whose supreme loyalty is to
        Christ as Lord
and who recognize all men as brothers in him.

The Lord's Prayer

Let us pray for racial reconciliation
112.   FATHER, who hast made all men in thy likeness
      and lovest all whom thou hast made,
  suffer not our family to separate itself from thee
      by building barriers of race and colour.
As thy Son our Saviour was born of a
        Hebrew Mother,
     but rejoiced in the faith of a Syrian woman
        and of a Roman soldier,
        welcomed the Greeks who sought him,
        and suffered a man from Africa
        to carry his cross,
  so teach us to regard the members of all races
      as fellow-heirs of the kingdom
      of Jesus Christ our Lord.

113.   WE PRAY THEE, O GOD,
      to breathe into the students of this day
      such brave magnanimity of thought and speech
        that righteousness in every land may speak
        with the clear voice of truth,
      and that the universities of all countries
        may not fail to raise up leaders
        bold and able to bring the nations
        into the ways of justice, brotherhood
         and peace.
  We ask it in his name
      who came to give life more abundantly,
       Jesus Christ our Lord.

114. GOD OF ALL NATIONS,
we pray thee for all the people of thy earth;
  for those who are consumed in mutual hatred
    and bitterness;
  for those who make war upon their neighbours;
  for those who tyrannously oppress;
  for those who groan under cruelty and subjection.
We beseech thee to teach mankind to live together
    in peace:
  no man exploiting the weak,
  no man hating the strong,
  each race working out its own destiny,
    unfettered, self-respecting, fearless.
Teach us to be worthy of freedom,
  free from social wrong,
  free from individual oppression
    and contempt,
  pure of heart and hand,
  despising none, defrauding none,
giving to all men—in all dealings of life—
the honour we owe to those who are thy children,
whatever their colour, their race or their caste.

AND NOW MAY THE BLESSING OF THE LORD
rest and remain upon all his people
    in every land, of every tongue.   *Amen.*

75

28. Leavening Society

The kingdom of heaven is like leaven which a woman took and hid in three measures of meal, till it was all leavened.

S. Matthew 13: 33

Do you not know that a little leaven ferments the whole lump of dough? Cleanse out the old leaven that you may be fresh dough, as you really are unleavened.

For Christ, our paschal lamb, has been sacrificed.

Let us, therefore, celebrate the festival, not with the old leaven, the leaven of malice and evil, but with the unleavened bread of sincerity and truth.

I Corinthians 5: 6-8

You are the salt of the earth; but if salt has lost its taste, how shall its saltness be restored? It is no longer good for anything except to be thrown out and trodden under foot by men.

You are the light of the world. A city set on a hill cannot be hid. Nor do men light a lamp and put it under a bushel, but on a stand, and it gives light to all in the house.

Let your light so shine before men, that they may see your good works and give glory to your Father who is in heaven.

S. Matthew 5: 13-16

Let us pray:

that in every nation Christians may be as salt, cleansing the national life, preserving all that is good, giving tone and character;

that Christians may give such selfless service to their own country that others may be brought to the Christian faith which inspires such insight and service.

115. WE PRAY THEE, O LORD, that thou wilt so reveal thyself in us, that through us men may be drawn to the love of thee. May the world not mould us today, but may we be strengthened to help mould the world; through Jesus Christ our Lord.

Let us pray for all who influence public opinion
116. ALMIGHTY GOD, who hast proclaimed thine eternal truth by the voice of prophets and evangelists: Direct and bless, we beseech thee, those who in this our generation speak where many listen and write what many read; that they may do their part in making the heart of the people wise, its mind sound, and its will righteous; to the honour of Jesus Christ our Lord.

Let us pray for the Church
117. O GOD OF UNCHANGEABLE POWER AND ETERNAL LIGHT,
   look favourably on thy whole Church,
   that wonderful and sacred mystery;
    and by the tranquil operation
    of thy perpetual providence,
   carry out the work of man's salvation;
   and let the whole world feel and see
    that things which were cast down
     are being raised up,
    that those which had grown old
     are being made new,
   and that all things are returning to perfection,
   through him from whom they took their origin,
    even Jesus Christ thy Son our Lord.

118. Now UNTO HIM that is able to do exceeding
    abundantly above all that we ask or think,
   according to the power that worketh in us,
  unto him be glory in the Church by Christ Jesus,
   throughout all ages, world without end. *Amen.*

V. ONE FAITH, ONE LORD, ONE CHURCH

29. The Bible

Whatever was written in former days was written for our
instruction, that by steadfastness and by the encourage-
ment of the scriptures we might have hope.   *Romans 15: 4*

You search the scriptures, because you think that in them
you have eternal life;
and it is they that bear witness to me.   *S. John 5: 39*

And he said to them,
O foolish men, and slow of heart to believe all that the
prophets have spoken! Was it not necessary that the
Christ should suffer these things and enter into his glory?
And beginning with Moses and all the prophets, he
interpreted to them in all the scriptures the things
concerning himself.   *S. Luke 24: 25-27*

But as for you, continue in what you have learned and
have firmly believed, knowing from whom you learned
it and how from childhood you have been acquainted
with the sacred writings which are able to instruct you
for salvation through faith in Christ Jesus.
All scripture is inspired by God and profitable for teaching,
for reproof, for correction, and for training in righteousness, that the man of God may be complete, equipped for
every good work.   *II Timothy 3: 14-17*

119.   To keep your Majesty ever mindful of the Law and
Gospel of God as the Rule for the whole life and
government of Christian Princes, we present you with
this Book, the most valuable thing that this world
affords. Here is Wisdom: This is the Royal Law:
These are the lively Oracles of God.

Let us thank God:

for the good news that has come to ourselves through the
Scriptures;

for the light and strength for daily living that come from
our study of the Bible;

for the translation of the Scriptures into over a thousand
languages, and for the work of translation all down
the ages;

for the Bible Societies who have been pioneers in the
translation and distribution of the Scriptures, and
whose aim it is that every man may have the Bible in
his own language at a price that he can afford;

that the Bible is the most loved, the best studied, and the
most widely distributed of all books.

Let us pray

120.   BLESSED LORD,
who has caused all holy Scriptures
to be written for our learning:
Grant that we may in such wise hear them,
read, mark, learn, and inwardly digest them,
that by patience,
and comfort of thy holy Word,
we may embrace and ever hold fast
the blessed hope of everlasting life,
which thou hast given us
in our Saviour Jesus Christ.

121. ALMIGHTY AND MOST MERCIFUL GOD,
    who hast given the Bible to be the revelation
        of thy great love to man,
        and of thy power and will to save him:
Grant that our study of it may not be made in vain
    by the callousness or carelessness of our hearts,
but that by it we may be confirmed in penitence,
        lifted to hope,
        made strong for service,
and, above all, filled with the true knowledge of thee
        and of thy Son Jesus Christ.

122. O GRACIOUS GOD AND MOST MERCIFUL FATHER,
    who hast vouchsafed us the rich and precious jewel
        of thy holy Word:
Assist us with thy Spirit
    that it may be written in our hearts
        to our everlasting comfort,
           to reform us,
    to renew us according to thine own image,
    to build us up into the perfect building
        of thy Christ,
    and to increase us in all heavenly virtues.
Grant this, O heavenly Father,
for the same Jesus Christ's sake.

123. THE GOD OF HOPE fill us with all joy and peace in
    believing, that we may abound in hope, in the
    power of the Holy Spirit. *Amen.*

30. The Body of Christ

Our Lord speaks of the relationship
between himself and his disciples

I am the true vine, and my Father is the vinedresser.

Every branch of mine that bears no fruit, he takes away, and every branch that does bear fruit he prunes, that it may bear more fruit.

You are already made clean by the word which I have spoken to you.

Abide in me, and I in you. As the branch cannot bear fruit by itself, unless it abides in the vine, neither can you, unless you abide in me.

I am the vine, you are the branches.

He who abides in me, and I in him, he it is that bears much fruit, for apart from me you can do nothing.

S. John 15: 1-5

St Paul speaks of the Church as the Body of Christ

For just as the body is one and has many members, and all the members of the body, though many, are one body, so it is with Christ.

For by one Spirit we were all baptized into one body— Jews or Greeks, slaves or free—and all were made to drink of one Spirit. . . .

Now you are the body of Christ and individually members of it.

I Corinthians 12: 12-14, 27

Each of us has his own work to do in the Church,
the Body of Christ

And his gifts were that some should be apostles,
　　　　　some prophets, some evangelists,
　　　　some pastors and teachers,
　　for the equipment of the saints,
　　for the work of ministry,
　　for building up the body of Christ,

until we all attain to the unity of the faith
  and of the knowledge of the Son of God,
    to mature manhood,
to the measure of the stature of the fullness of Christ.

Ephesians 4: 11-13

Let us meditate upon:
  the Church as the visible organ through which the
    ascended Christ now lives and works among men as
    he once did through his human body;
  the things which Christ did while he was here on earth—
    revealing God;
    healing men;
    bringing them forgiveness;
    loving them; dying for them;
    rescuing them from the power of evil;
    cleansing and strengthening human nature.
  Christ as the head whom all the members of the body
      obey;
    disobedience in any of the limbs means paralysis.
  Our relationship to one another as fellow-members of the
    body, all working in harmony for the whole body in
    obedience to the Head.

Let us pray
124.   GRANT, O LORD GOD, that thy Church,
            as it hath one Foundation and one Head,
          may verily and indeed be one body,
              holding one faith, proclaiming one truth,
              and following one Lord in holiness of living and
                love,
            even thy Son our Saviour Jesus Christ.

125. ALMIGHTY AND EVER-LIVING GOD,
    we most heartily thank thee that we are
    very members incorporate in the mystical body
        of thy Son,
    which is the blessed company of all faithful people.
And we most humbly beseech thee, O heavenly
        Father,
    so to assist us with thy grace,
    that we may continue in that holy fellowship,
        and do all such good works
        as thou hast prepared for us to walk in;
    through Jesus Christ our Lord.

126. ETERNAL GOD,
    look mercifully upon the broken body of thy
        Church.
        Draw its members unto thee
            and one to another
            by the bands of thy love;
        that its restored unity may bring healing
            to the nations,
        and the life of mankind may glorify thee;
        through Jesus Christ our Lord.

The Lord's Prayer

127. ETERNAL FATHER,
    of whom the whole family in heaven and earth is
        named:
        Unite us, as we worship thee here,
            with all who in far-off places
            are lifting up their hands and hearts to thee;
        that thy Church throughout the world,
            with the Church in heaven,
        may offer up one sacrifice of thanksgiving;
        to the praise and honour of thy holy Name.

83

31. As I have loved you

The two great commandments
> You shall love the Lord your God with all your heart,
> and with all your soul, and with all your mind, and
> with all your strength. The second is this,
> You shall love your neighbor as yourself.
> There is no other commandment greater than these.
>
> *S. Mark 12: 30-31*

> A new commandment I give to you, that you love one
> another; even as I have loved you, that you also love
> one another.
>
> *S. John 13: 34*

> Love is very patient, very kind. Love knows no jealousy;
> love makes no parade, gives itself no airs, is never rude,
> never selfish, never irritated, never resentful;
>> love is never glad when others go wrong,
> love is gladdened by goodness, always slow to expose,
> always eager to believe the best, always hopeful, always
> patient.
> Love never disappears.
>
> *I Cor. 13: 4-8 (Moffatt)*

Meditation
> Our Lord commands us not only to love our fellowmen
> as ourselves, but to love them as he has loved us.
> God's love for us is completely self-giving, without any
> thought of our worth to God or of our being worthy of
> love; love even for the loveless and unlovable.
> This selfless love is the gift of the Holy Spirit; St Paul
> calls it the greatest of all gifts. We should desire it
> earnestly, and unceasingly ask God to give it to us.
> It is love which will win men to God more than anything
> else.

128. O LORD, who hast taught us that all our doings without charity are nothing worth: Send thy Holy Ghost, and pour into our hearts that most excellent gift of charity, the very bond of peace and of all virtues, without which whosoever liveth is counted dead before thee: Grant this for thine only Son Jesus Christ's sake.

129. LORD, if we love thee
    for the pleasure that we receive
        then we but love ourselves;
    But if we love thee
        to do thee pleasure again,
    then let us rejoice to obey thee,
    and, for thy sake, to love our brethren;
        them that are good
            to support them in goodness,
        them that are ignorant or careless or evil
            to draw them to good,
    to be unto all our neighbours
        as Christ unto us; for his mercy's sake.

130. O LORD, grant us to love thee:
    grant that we may love those that love thee;
    grant that we may do the deeds that win thy love.

A prayer of Mohammed

The Lord's Prayer

131. O CHRIST OUR GOD, dwell in our hearts,
    that we, being rooted and grounded in love,
    and understanding with all the saints
what is the breadth and length and depth and height;
    and knowing the love of God which passeth
        knowledge
        may be filled with all thy fullness. *Amen.*

32. *Even so send I you*

Jesus said to them,
> Peace be with you. As the Father has sent me, even so I send you.

And when he had said this, he breathed on them, and said,
> Receive the Holy Spirit. If you forgive the sins of any, they are forgiven; if you retain the sins of any, they are retained.

S. John 20: 21-23

And Jesus came and said to them,
> All authority in heaven and on earth has been given to me. Go therefore and make disciples of all nations, baptizing them in the name of the Father and of the Son and of the Holy Spirit, teaching them to observe all that I have commanded you; and lo, I am with you always, to the close of the age.

S. Matthew 28: 18-20

And he said to them,
> Go into all the world and preach the gospel to the whole creation.

S. Mark 16: 15

Thus it is written . . . that repentance and forgiveness of sins should be preached in his name to all nations, beginning from Jerusalem.

S. Luke 24: 46-47

But you shall receive power when the Holy Spirit has come upon you; and you shall be my witnesses in Jerusalem and in all Judea and Samaria and to the end of the earth.

Acts 1: 8

Reflect:

All four evangelists record our Lord's command to take part in his mission to the world.

It is the Risen Lord, to whom all power and authority are given, who sends his apostles out.

The mission is to start where the disciples are and spread outwards: where each Christian is—his own country—neighbouring countries—every country;

not only every country, but every area of thought and society.

We do not go alone: Lo, I am with you alway.

We go as bearers of good news, telling men what God has done, inviting them to claim God's gracious promises.

Let us pray

132. O GOD, mighty to save, infinite in compassion towards the nations that know thee not, and the tongues which cannot speak thy name: We humbly thank thee that thou hast made the Church of thy dear Son the chariot of the gospel, to tell it out among the nations that thou art king, and to bear thy love unto the world's end: and for all thy servants who counted not their lives dear unto them on this employment, and for all peoples newly praising thee, we praise and bless thee, Father, Son, and Holy Spirit, one Lord and God for ever.

133. BESTOW THY BLESSING, we beseech thee, O Lord, upon thy Church and thy ministers everywhere. May increasing multitudes hear thy word, receive it, and live by it. May its power be seen more and more in the lives of them that believe.

So work thy great work, Almighty God, in this our country, and in this our generation, that the

doubter may be convinced, the wavering established, the sinful converted and the gainsayer
silenced;

and grant that at the last, according to thy blessed
word of prophecy, the Lord may be king over all
the earth, one Lord and his name one; through
Jesus Christ our Lord.

The Lord's Prayer

Thanksgiving for the progress of the Gospel

134. THOU ART WORTHY, O LORD, to receive power,
and riches
and wisdom and strength,
and honour and glory, and blessing.
Blessed be thy glorious name that thy word has
sounded forth
not only in Jerusalem and Antioch, in Athens and
in Rome;
but in every place the faith of Christ is spread abroad.
All glory be to thee.

For the light of thy everlasting gospel,
sent to every nation, and kindred,
and tongue, and people,
shining so long amongst ourselves;
for thy Church, the pillar and ground of the truth,
against which the gates of hell have not prevailed;
for thy gracious word of promise,
that they that be wise shall shine
as the brightness of the firmament,
and they that turn many to righteousness
as the stars for ever and ever,
All glory be to thee.

135. GOD BE MERCIFUL unto us and bless us;
and give us grace to know his will,
and strength to do it,
for Jesus Christ's sake. *Amen.*

88

33. *That they may be one*

I have manifested thy name to the men whom thou gavest
me out of the world; thine they were, and thou gavest
them to me, and they have kept thy word. . . .

I am praying for them; I am not praying for the world
but for those whom thou hast given me, for they
are thine; . . .

And now I am no more in the world, but they are in the
world, and I am coming to thee.

Holy Father, keep them in thy name which thou hast
given me, that they may be one, even as we are
one . . . that they may all be one; even as thou,
Father, art in me, and I in thee, that they also may
be in us, so that the world may believe that thou
hast sent me.   *S. John 17: 6, 9, 11, 21*

There is one body and one Spirit, just as you were called
to the one hope that belongs to your call, one Lord,
one faith, one baptism, one God and Father of us all,
who is above all and through all and in all.

Ephesians 4: 4-6

A new commandment I give to you, that you love one
another; even as I have loved you, that you also love
one another.

By this all men will know that you are my disciples, if you
have love for one another.   *S. John 13: 34-35*

136.   O LORD JESUS CHRIST, who didst say to thine apostles,
By this shall all men know that ye are my disciples,
if ye have love one to another:
Heal our divisions, and make us one:
one soul and body in thee:
that men may know us for thy true children;
and believe in thee through us.

Let us confess:

    our lack of charity and brotherliness to Christians of other
        denominations

    our past indifference to the need for unity

    our denominational pride and prejudice

    our responsibility through disunity for delaying the
        conversion of the world.

Let us pray:

    that our search for unity may be based on truth as well
        as on goodwill and love

    for the Holy Spirit's guidance of all efforts for Church
        union

    for all Churches, that each abandoning error and
        prejudice may bring its gifts to the one Holy, Catholic
        and Apostolic Church.

Let us thank God:

    for the stirring of conscience about our lack of unity

    for the growing realization of our common faith

    for the growing volume of prayer that God will show the
        divided parts of the Church the way back to unity

    for the Younger Churches who have spoken with such
        conviction of the need for unity

    for the ecumenical movement, through which Christians
        of many denominations are striving to find that unity
        which Christ wills for his Church.

The Lord's Prayer

137.   O GOD, who by thy Son Jesus Christ
        dost call the children of thy Church
           into a great and holy unity,
           even as he is one with thee:
        Turn us again, we beseech thee,
        that we may redeem the years of division,
        and recover in thee what we have lost of ourselves;

through the same Jesus Christ our Lord,
    who liveth and reigneth with thee
    in the unity of the Holy Spirit,
    God, for ever and ever.

138. O LORD JESUS CHRIST, who didst say to thine apostles,
    Peace I leave with you, my peace I give unto you:
        Regard not our sins, but the faith of thy Church,
            and grant it that peace and unity
            which is agreeable to thy will;
                who livest and reignest
                with the Father and the Holy Spirit,
                one God, world without end.

139. NOW UNTO HIM that is able to do exceeding
                abundantly
            above all that we ask or think,
            according to the power that worketh in us,
        unto him be glory in the Church
            and in Christ Jesus
        unto all generations for ever and ever.   *Amen.*

34. Growing Together

Christ's Will for his Church

His gifts were that some should be apostles, some prophets, some evangelists, some pastors and teachers, for the equipment of the saints, for the work of ministry, for building up the body of Christ, until we all attain to the unity of the faith and of the knowledge of the Son of God, to mature manhood, to the measure of the stature of the fullness of Christ;

so that we may no longer be children, tossed to and fro and carried about with every wind of doctrine, by the cunning of men, by their craftiness in deceitful wiles.

Rather, speaking the truth in love, we are to grow up in every way into him who is the head, into Christ, from whom the whole body, joined and knit together by every joint with which it is supplied, when each part is working properly, makes bodily growth and upbuilds itself in love.

Ephesians 4: 11-16

Let us thank God:

for the growing concern for unity which has developed in recent years;

for the spirit of unity which develops among Christians when there is a strong sense of mission;

for God's over-ruling of our divisions to preserve or recover aspects of his truth, to save souls, and to build up communities who worship him;

for the pioneer part played in bringing Christians together by the Bible Societies, the Evangelical Alliance, the Y.M.C.A. and Y.W.C.A., and the Student Christian Movement;

for the Missionary Conference, Edinburgh 1910, and for the International Missionary Council and many National Christian Councils which sprang out of it;

for the founding of the World Council of Churches at Amsterdam in 1948, and for many National Councils of Churches;

for the Christian encounter that has taken place in these
Councils, and for many union institutions and schemes
of unity which have developed in different parts of the
world;

for the growth of fellowship and mutual responsibility
among the Churches, especially in time of war.

The Lord's Prayer

Let us pray:

for a deeper understanding of Christ's relationship to his
Church, and his will for it;

for honest penitence about the perpetuation of our divisions and any sectarian spirit still existing;

for churches which are too comfortable or too self-
centred, that they may realize their need for conversion,
for a greater concern about unity, and for more costly
commitment to the world mission of the Church;

for the guidance of all who are working to achieve
Christian unity, especially for those studying the
problems of faith and order;

for a growing realization of the influence of social and
cultural differences in causing divisions, and for a
readiness to discuss our differing convictions openly;

for the guidance of the Holy Spirit for the International
Missionary Council and the World Council of Churches
and for all National Councils of Churches;

for the inspiration of the Holy Spirit in local co-operation
between Churches, that, growing up into Christ, we
may attain to unity of faith, worship and mission;

for more earnest and faithful prayer for unity.

140. ETERNAL AND MERCIFUL GOD, who art the God of
peace and not of discord: Have mercy upon thy
Church, divided in thy service; and grant that we,
seeking unity in Christ, and in the truth of thy holy
word, with one mind and one mouth may glorify
thee, the Father of our Lord Jesus Christ. *Amen.*

35. *To sum up all things in Christ*

For God has made known to us in all wisdom and insight
    the mystery of his will,
according to his purpose which he set forth in Christ
    as a plan for the fullness of time,
to unite all things in him, things in heaven and things on
    earth.

Ephesians 1 : 9-10

For the creation waits with eager longing
    for the revealing of the sons of God;
for the creation was subjected to futility,
      not of its own will
but by the will of him who subjected it in hope;
because the creation itself will be set free
      from its bondage to decay
    and obtain the glorious liberty
      of the children of God.

Romans 8 : 19-21

Meditation

All things shall find their goal and perfection in Christ.
No man will find his highest good until he has come face
    to face with Christ and accepted Christ's claims.
Not only men, but the whole creation shall find its goal
    in Christ. But this depends on all men accepting their
    freedom as sons of God and living as such.

Let us pray:

that all spheres of man's life and work may be brought
    under the rule of Christ:
      politics and government, trade and industry,
      management and labour, agriculture and farming,
      science and invention, art and literature,
          personal relationships.

141.   BLESSED BE THOU, O GOD,
who hast declared that it is thine eternal purpose
to gather in one all things in Christ.
Worthy art thou to receive honour and power and
glory,
for the great love wherewith thou hast loved all
mankind,
and hast delivered us from the powers of darkness,
and brought us into the kingdom of thy Son.

142.   YEA, O LORD CHRIST,
in thee hath it been the good pleasure of God
to sum up all things,
the things in the heavens
and the things upon the earth:
and through thee, through the blood of thy cross,
to reconcile all things unto himself,
whether things upon the earth
or things in the heavens:
that in thy name, Lord Jesus,
every knee should bow,
of things in heaven and things in earth
and things under the earth:
and that every tongue should confess that thou art
Lord,
to the glory of God the Father.

The Lord's Prayer

143.   Now UNTO HIM that is able to stablish you
according to the eternal gospel of Jesus Christ—
made known unto all the nations,
for their obedience to the faith—
to the only wise God be the glory
for ever and ever. *Amen.*

VI. HIS WITNESSES

36. Apostles

And he went up into the hills, and called to him those
whom he desired; and they came to him.
And he appointed twelve, to be with him, and to be sent
out to preach and have authority to cast out demons.

S. Mark 3: 13-14

These twelve Jesus sent out, charging them. . . . Preach as
you go, saying, The kingdom of heaven is at hand. Heal
the sick, raise the dead, cleanse lepers, cast out demons.
You received without pay, give without pay. Take no
gold, nor silver, nor copper in your belts, no bag for your
journey, nor two tunics, nor sandals, nor a staff; for the
laborer deserves his food.   *S. Matthew 10: 5, 7-10*

And Jesus came and said to them:
All authority in heaven and on earth has been given to
me. Go therefore and make disciples of all nations,
baptizing them in the name of the Father and of the
Son and of the Holy Spirit, teaching them to observe
all that I have commanded you; and lo, I am with you
always, to the close of the age.   *S. Matthew 28: 18-20*

144. PRAISE BE TO THY NAME for the first disciples who
were sent forth to proclaim the coming of thy
kingdom;

for the apostles who, in obedience to thy word, carried the gospel to many lands;
for the messengers, known and unknown, who brought the good tidings to our own shores
and for all who have gone to the ends of the world with the joyful news.
Praise be to thee.

145. O Almighty God, who hast built thy Church upon the foundation of the apostles and prophets,
Jesus Christ himself being the head corner-stone: Grant us so to be joined together
in unity of spirit by their doctrine,
that we may be made an holy temple acceptable unto thee;
through Jesus Christ our Lord.

146. O Lord Jesus Christ, who didst send forth thy first disciples to proclaim thy kingdom, and to teach thy commandments:
Give to us, thy disciples this day, such an understanding of the word, that we may teach to others what we have been taught of thee; to the glory of thy name, and the spread of thy kingdom.

Remembering that we can have no share in Christ unless we share in his mission to the world,
let us pray for an ever-deepening sense of mission throughout the whole Church, saying,

Our Father . . .

147. We give thanks to thee, O Lord God, Father Almighty, together with thy Son our Lord and Saviour Jesus Christ, and the Holy Spirit.
All nations offer praise and thanksgiving unto thee, O Lord, from the rising of the sun unto the going down thereof, from the north and from the south, for great is thy name in all nations. *Amen.*

37. Saints and Martyrs

After this I looked, and behold, a great multitude which no man could number, from every nation, from all tribes and peoples and tongues, standing before the throne and before the Lamb, clothed in white robes, with palm branches in their hands, and crying out with a loud voice,

> Salvation belongs to our God who sits upon the throne, and to the Lamb!

And all the angels stood round the throne and round the elders and the four living creatures, and they fell on their faces before the throne and worshipped God, saying,

> Amen! Blessing and glory and wisdom and thanksgiving and honor and power and might be to our God for ever and ever! Amen.

Revelation 7 : 9-12

Therefore, since we are surrounded by so great a cloud of witnesses, let us also lay aside every weight, and sin which clings so closely, and let us run with perseverance the race that is set before us, looking to Jesus the pioneer and perfecter of our faith, who for the joy that was set before him endured the cross, despising the shame, and is seated at the right hand of the throne of God.

Hebrews 12 : 1-2

Let us pray

148.   PRAISE BE TO THEE, O GOD,

> for the noble army of martyrs all through the ages,
> and for all converts to the faith who have sealed their witness with their blood;
> for the mighty company who now praise thy name,
> out of every kindred and nation and tongue.

All praise be to thee, thou king of saints.

149. ALMIGHTY AND EVERLASTING GOD, who dost enkindle
the flame of thy love in the hearts of the saints;
grant to our minds the same faith and power of
love; that as we rejoice in their triumphs, we may
profit by their examples; through Jesus Christ
our Lord.

150. O KING, ETERNAL, IMMORTAL, INVISIBLE,
who in the righteousness of thy saints
hast given us an example of godly life,
and in their blessedness a glorious pledge
of the hope of our calling,
we beseech thee that, being compassed about
with so great a cloud of witnesses,
we may run with patience the race that is set before us,
and with them receive the crown of glory
that fadeth not away;
through Jesus Christ our Lord.

151. ALMIGHTY GOD, by whose grace and power thy holy
martyrs
triumphed over suffering and death:
Inspire us, we pray thee, with the same faith,
that, enduring affliction and waxing valiant in fight,
we with them may secure
the crown of everlasting life;
through Jesus Christ our Lord.

*Remembering our Christian brethren throughout the world who are
suffering for their faith, let us say together for them*

The Lord's Prayer

152. THE GOD OF ALL GRACE,
who hath called us unto his eternal glory
by Christ Jesus,
after that we have suffered awhile,
make us perfect, stablish, strengthen, settle us,
to him be glory and dominion for ever and ever.
Amen.

38. Everyday Saints

All thy works shall give thanks to thee, O Lord,
    and all thy saints shall bless thee!
They shall speak of the glory of thy kingdom,
    and tell of thy power,
to make known to the sons of men thy mighty deeds,
    and the glorious splendor of thy kingdom.

Psalm 145: 10-12

Paul, called by the will of God to be an apostle of Christ
    Jesus, and our brother Sosthenes, To the church of God
    which is at Corinth, to those sanctified in Christ Jesus,
    called to be saints together with all those who in every
    place call on the name of our Lord Jesus Christ, both
    their Lord and ours:
Grace to you and peace from God our Father and the
    Lord Jesus Christ.

I Corinthians 1: 1-3

Not every one who says to me, Lord, Lord, shall enter the
    kingdom of heaven, but he who does the will of my
    Father who is in heaven.

S. Matthew 7: 21

Let us remember
    that to become saints we have only
        to be what God wants us to be
        and to do what God wants us to do;
        to forget ourselves and never to forget God;
            the need for
    perfect simplicity with regard to ourselves;
    perfect contentment with all that comes our way;
    perfect peace of mind in utter self-forgetfulness.
    This becomes easier as we realize
      the utter greatness, and goodness,
      and all-ness of God.

153. WE THANK THEE, O GOD, for the saints of all ages;
for those who in times of darkness kept the lamp of
faith burning;
for the great souls who saw visions of larger truth and
dared to declare it;
for the multitude of quiet and gracious souls whose
presence has purified and sanctified the world;
and for those known and loved by us, who have
passed from this earthly fellowship into the fuller
light of life with thee.

154. O ALMIGHTY GOD, who has knit together thine elect
in one communion and fellowship, in the mystical
body of thy Son Christ our Lord: Grant us grace
so to follow thy blessed saints in all virtuous and
godly living, that we may come to those unspeak-
able joys, which thou hast prepared for them that
unfeignedly love thee; through Jesus Christ our
Lord.

155. O LORD, who in every age dost reveal thyself to the
childlike and lowly of heart, and from every race
dost write names in thy book of life:
Give us the simplicity and faith of thy saints, that
loving thee above all things, we may be what
thou wouldst have us be and do what thou
wouldst have us do.
So may we be numbered with thy saints and enter
with them into eternal joy and glory, through
Jesus Christ, our Saviour.

The Lord's Prayer

156. GREAT AND MARVELLOUS are thy works, O Lord God,
the Almighty;
righteous and true are thy ways, thou king of saints.
Amen.

39. Ministers of Christ

Our Lord's description of his own ministry
>The Spirit of the Lord is upon me, because he has anointed me to preach good news to the poor.
>
>He has sent me to proclaim release to the captives and recovering of sight to the blind, to set at liberty those who are oppressed, to proclaim the acceptable year of the Lord.

S. Luke 4: 18-19

The Ascended Lord's provision for his Church
>But grace was given to each of us according to the measure of Christ's gift. . . .
>
>And his gifts were that some should be apostles, some prophets, some evangelists, some pastors and teachers, for the equipment of the saints, for the work of ministry, for building up the body of Christ,
>
>until we all attain to the unity of the faith and of the knowledge of the Son of God, to mature manhood, to the measure of the stature of the fullness of Christ.

Ephesians 4: 7, 11-13

Ministers of the Word and Sacraments
>So those who received Peter's word were baptized, and there were added that day about three thousand souls. And they devoted themselves to the apostles' teaching and fellowship, to the breaking of bread and the prayers.

Acts 2: 41-42

Let us pray:
>for the ministers of all communions,
>>of every race and country,
>
>that they may be holy and humble in heart,
>>full of the Spirit, and of wisdom and faith,
>>faithful ministers of the Word and Sacraments;

for all ordained ministers in specialist posts—
  in education, industry, church administration,
  literature production and ecumenical relationships;
that the Holy Spirit may show us the way
  to a ministry which shall be recognized
  throughout the whole Church;
that Christians may support their ministers
  by regular prayer and by the expectation
  to receive through them the word of the Lord.

The Lord's Prayer

157. ALMIGHTY GOD, the giver of all good gifts,
  who of thy divine providence
    hast appointed divers orders in thy Church:
Give thy grace, we humbly beseech thee,
  to all those who are called
  to any office and administration in the same;
and so replenish them with the truth of thy doctrine,
  and endue them with innocency of life,
that they may faithfully serve before thee,
  to the glory of thy great Name,
  and the benefit of thy holy Church;
through Jesus Christ our Lord.

158. WE PRAY THEE, LORD, for all who minister in thy
        name.
  Strengthen them in time of weakness and trial,
    and direct them in all their work.
  Give unto them the spirit of power, and of love,
        and of sound mind,
  that in all their work they may set forth thy glory,
    and set forward the salvation of souls;
  that so the nations may become thine inheritance,
  and the uttermost parts of the earth thy possession;
    through Jesus Christ our Lord.

159. GRANT, O GOD, we beseech thee, that the same mind
   may be in all the ministers of thy Church,
   that was in Christ Jesus;
       his self-forgetting humility;
       his interest in common things;
       his love for common people;
       his compassion for the fallen;
       his tolerance with the mistaken;
       his patience with the slow;
   and in all their work and converse
   make them continually sensitive to thy guidance
       and ready for thy will,
       through Jesus Christ our Lord.

160. UNTO HIM that loved us,
   and washed us from our sins, in his own blood,
   and hath made us kings and priests unto God,
       to him be glory and dominion,
       for ever and ever. *Amen.*

40. A Royal Priesthood

Now therefore, if you will obey my voice and keep my covenant, you shall be my own possession among all peoples;
for all the earth is mine, and you shall be to me a kingdom of priests and a holy nation.

Exodus 19: 5, 6

You shall be called the priests of the Lord, men shall speak of you as the ministers of our God.

Isaiah 61: 6

But you are a chosen race, a royal priesthood, a holy nation, God's own people, that you may declare the wonderful deeds of him who called you out of darkness into his marvelous light.

I Peter 2: 9

Meditation

These words of Scripture are addressed
    to all the people of God;
all have their part in worship, in witness,
    and in bringing other people to God:
    all have a responsibility for others.
The real battles of the faith today are being fought
    in factories, shops, offices, and farms,
    in political parties and government agencies,
        in countless homes,
    in the press, radio and television,
    in the relationship of nations.
Often it is said that the Church should go
        into these spheres,
but the fact is that the Church is already there
    in the persons of its laity.

161. ALMIGHTY AND EVERLASTING GOD,
    by whose Spirit the whole body of the Church
        is governed and sanctified:
    Receive our supplications and prayers,
        which we offer before thee
    for all estates of men in thy holy Church,
        that every member of the same,
        in his vocation and ministry,
    may truly and godly serve thee;
through our Lord and Saviour Jesus Christ.

162. WE COMMEND TO THEE, ALMIGHTY GOD, the whole
    Christian Church throughout the world.
    Bless all in every place who call on the name of our
    Lord Jesus Christ.
    May the grace and power of the Holy Spirit fill every
    member, so that all the company of thy faithful
    people may bear witness for thee on the earth.
    Look in mercy on the errors and confusions of our
    time, and draw the hearts of believers nearer to
    the Lord Jesus Christ.
    If it be good in thy sight, heal the outward divisions
    of thy people, disposing the wills of all to a true
    union of order in the truth, for the work of the one
    Lord.
    And above all we pray for the unity of the Spirit,
    through whom alone we are guided into all truth.

163. HERE, O LORD, WE OFFER and present unto thee
        ourselves, our souls and bodies,
    to be a reasonable, holy and living sacrifice;
        humbly beseeching thee
    that thou wilt accept this our offering,
    and use it for the work of thy kingdom,
    and the making known of thy love to all mankind;
        through Jesus Christ our Lord.

164. LOOK DOWN, O LORD, upon our fellow-Christians
who are scattered abroad,
and quicken in them the fire of thy love,
that realizing the blessedness of the true faith,
they may become living witnesses for thee,
in word and deed,
unto the people amongst whom they dwell;
who livest and reignest
with the Father and the Holy Spirit,
one God for ever and ever.

Let us pray especially for the lay people
who serve God in many kinds of church work:
elders and deacons, churchwardens and treasurers,
women workers, Sunday School teachers,
secretaries, sidesmen, vergers,
choir members, organists and many others.

The Lord's Prayer

165. GO FORTH INTO THE WORLD in peace;
be of good courage; hold fast that which is good;
render to no man evil for evil;
strengthen the fainthearted;
support the weak, help the afflicted;
honour all men;
love and serve the Lord,
rejoicing in the power of the Holy Spirit.
And the blessing of God Almighty,
the Father, the Son, and the Holy Ghost,
be upon you,
and remain with you for ever. *Amen.*

41. Community Life

Let us thank God for all who have sacrificed the joy of ordinary family life that they may serve God in religious communities.

Let us pray for God's blessing on their worship and work, and rejoice in our oneness with them in working for the furtherance of God's kingdom on earth.

I. For all Brotherhoods and Sisterhoods living in Community

You did not choose me, but I chose you and appointed you that you should go and bear fruit and that your fruit should abide.

S. John 15 : 16

They are not of the world, even as I am not of the world.

S. John 17 : 16

My God will supply every need of yours according to his riches in glory in Christ Jesus.

Philippians 4 : 19

166. O LORD JESUS CHRIST, who hast promised to restore an hundredfold in spiritual blessing whatsoever is forsaken for thy sake: Uphold and enlighten thy servants whom thou hast called to leave all and follow thee; accept their prayer and fasting, sanctify their labours, and be their defence against all perils; who livest and reignest with the Father and the Holy Ghost, ever one God, world without end.

167. BLESSED ARE THEY that dwell in thy house:
          they will be alway praising thee.
      Blessed is the man whose strength is in thee,
          in whose heart are thy ways;
      who going through the vale of misery use it for a well,
          and the pools are filled with water.
      They will go from strength to strength,
      and unto the God of gods appeareth every one of
          them in Sion.

II. For Ashrams and similar religious Communities

Now the company of those who believed were of one
    heart and soul, and no one said that any of the things
    which he possessed was his own, but they had every-
    thing in common.

Acts 4: 32

168. BLESS, WE BESEECH THEE, O LORD, thy servants who
          have joined themselves together for the furtherance
          of thy kingdom upon earth; that they may be
          zealous in their labours for thee and fervent in their
          love for one another; through Jesus Christ our Lord.

169. I will declare thy Name unto my brethren;
          in the midst of the congregation will I praise thee.
          O praise the Lord, ye that fear him;
          magnify him, all ye of the seed of Jacob,
          and fear him, all ye seed of Israel.
      My praise is of thee in the great congregation;
          my vows will I perform in the sight of them
                  that fear him;
          the poor shall eat and be satisfied;
          they that seek after the Lord shall praise him;
          your heart shall live for ever.
      All the ends of the world shall remember themselves,
          and be turned unto the Lord.

III. For Contemplative Communities

How lovely is thy dwelling place, O Lord of hosts!
My soul longs, yea, faints for the courts of the Lord;
    my heart and flesh sing for joy
    to the living God. . . .
For a day in thy courts is better than a thousand . . .

Psalm 84: 1, 2, 10

170.   O God who art the exceeding great reward
      of those who seek thee,
  prosper the endeavours of those whom thou hast •
      called
    to devote themselves entirely to thy worship:
  cherish and guide them by the inspiration
      of thy Holy Spirit,
    that they may be truly centred upon thee,
  and worship thee in sincerity and truth;
    through Jesus Christ our Lord.

171.   O GOD, THOU ART MY GOD, early will I seek thee.
    My soul thirsteth for thee, my flesh also longeth after
      thee
      in a barren and dry land where no water is.
  Thus have I looked for thee in holiness,
    that I might behold thy power and glory;
 for thy loving-kindness is better than the life itself,
      my lips shall praise thee.

The Lord's Prayer

172.   O GOD, who has prepared for them that love thee
such good things as pass man's understanding:
pour into our hearts such love toward thee, that
we loving thee above all things, may obtain thy
promises, which exceed all that we can desire;
through Jesus Christ our Lord. *Amen.*

42. *Training for the Ministry*

In the year that King Uzziah died I saw the Lord sitting
  upon a throne, high and lifted up;
  and his train filled the temple.
Above him stood the seraphim; each had six wings:
  with two he covered his face, and with two he covered
  his feet, and with two he flew.
  And one called to another and said:
    Holy, holy, holy is the Lord of hosts;
    the whole earth is full of his glory.
And the foundations of the thresholds shook at the voice of
  him who called, and the house was filled with smoke.
And I said: Woe is me! For I am lost; for I am a man of
    unclean lips, and I dwell in the midst of a people of
    unclean lips;
    for my eyes have seen the King, the Lord of hosts!
Then flew one of the seraphim to me,
  having in his hand a burning coal which he had taken
  with tongs from the altar. And he touched my mouth,
  and said:
    Behold, this has touched your lips;
    your guilt is taken away, and your sin forgiven.
And I heard the voice of the Lord saying,
  Whom shall I send, and who will go for us?
Then I said, Here I am! Send me.

Isaiah 6: 1-8

When he saw the crowds, he had compassion for them,
  because they were harassed and helpless, like sheep
  without a shepherd.
Then he said to his disciples,
    The harvest is plentiful, but the laborers are few; pray
    therefore the Lord of the harvest to send out laborers
    into his harvest.

S. Matthew 9: 36-38

But you, beloved, build yourselves up on your most holy
    faith;
pray in the Holy Spirit;
keep yourselves in the love of God;
wait for the mercy of our Lord Jesus Christ unto eternal life.

Jude: 20-21

Let us pray:
    for those who are being trained for the ministry of the
        Church in our own country and in other countries;
    for theological colleges, that they may have all that is
        necessary in staff and buildings;
    for the guidance of the Holy Spirit in all plans for the
        deepening and developing of theological training in the
        lands of the younger churches;
    that the necessary books for training the ministry may be
        made available in all languages;
    that the Holy Spirit may guide the Church in new plans
        for calling and training a voluntary ministry to assist
        the whole-time ministers, so that every Christian
        group may have an adequate ministry of both Word
        and Sacrament.

The Lord's Prayer

173.   WE PRAY, O LORD, for thy blessing
            upon all who are being trained
            for the ministry of thy Church in every land.
        Take from them all pride and self-conceit,
            all thought of worldly advancement.
        May their wills be wholly surrendered unto thee;
        fill them with thy Spirit, that they may go forth
            inspired with zeal for thy glory,
            in the power of our Lord Jesus Christ.

174. O ALMIGHTY GOD, look mercifully upon the world
                which thou hast redeemed
                by the blood of thy dear Son,
        and incline the hearts of many to offer themselves
                for the sacred ministry of thy Church;
                so that by their labours
                thy light may shine in the darkness,
        and the coming of thy kingdom may be hastened
                by the perfecting of thine elect;
                through the same Jesus Christ our Lord.

A prayer for theological colleges:

175. O EVERLASTING GOD, adored and served by the hosts
        of heaven yet choosing to use men upon earth to
        lead the praises of thy creatures and to bestow upon
        thy people mercy and forgiveness:
    Graciously pour we pray thee thy blessing upon
        theological colleges;
    Preserve and renew the customs and teaching given
        and observed therein, that they who are there to
        learn and be trained may by thee be strengthened
        in loyalty and love, disciplined and nurtured by
        thy Word and Sacraments,
    and when the time is come, being ordained ministers
        of the New Covenant, go forth into the world and
        advance thy glory and the welfare of thy children;
    through thine eternally begotten and beloved Son,
    Jesus Christ our Lord and Saviour.

176. TEACH US, GOOD LORD, to serve thee as thou deservest;
                to give and not to count the cost;
                to fight and not to heed the wounds;
                to toil and not to seek for rest;
                to labour and to ask for no reward,
        save that of knowing that we do thy will;
                through Jesus Christ our Lord. *Amen.*

113

VII. HIS KINGDOM

43. Our Citizenship is in Heaven

Our commonwealth is in heaven, and from it we await a
Savior, the Lord Jesus Christ, who will change our lowly
body to be like his glorious body, by the power which
enables him even to subject all things to himself.

Philippians 3: 20-21

If then you have been raised with Christ, seek the things
that are above, where Christ is, seated at the right hand
of God.
Set your minds on things that are above, not on things that
are on earth. For you have died, and your life is hid
with Christ in God.
When Christ who is our life appears, then you also will
appear with him in glory. *Colossians 3: 1-4*

By faith Abraham sojourned in the land of promise . . .
For he looked forward to the city which has foundations,
whose builder and maker is God. *Hebrews 11: 9-10*

An ancient act of faith
177.   The Lord is my shepherd, therefore can I lack nothing.
He shall feed me in a green pasture,
and lead me forth beside the waters of comfort.
He shall convert my soul, and bring me forth
in the paths of righteousness, for his Name's sake.
Yea, though I walk through the valley of the
shadow of death,
I will fear no evil, for thou art with me . . .
I will dwell in the house of the Lord for ever.

178. O God, the protector of all that trust in thee,
without whom nothing is strong, nothing is holy:
    Increase and multiply upon us thy mercy;
    that, thou being our ruler and guide,
    we may so pass through things temporal,
    that we finally lose not the things eternal:
Grant this, O heavenly Father,
for Jesus Christ's sake our Lord.

179. O God, who rulest the world from everlasting to
        everlasting:
Speak to our hearts when courage fails, and we faint
        for fear;
        when our love grows cold,
    and there is distress of nations upon the earth.
Keep us resolute and steadfast in the things
        that cannot be shaken,
        abounding in hope
and knowing that our labour is not in vain in thee.

180. O Lord, support us all the day long of this troublous
        life,
    until the shadows lengthen, and the evening comes,
        and the busy world is hushed,
    the fever of life is over, and our work is done.
Then, Lord, in thy mercy, grant us safe lodging,
    a holy rest, and peace at the last;
        through Jesus Christ our Lord.

The Lord's Prayer

181. May the eternal God bless and keep us,
guard our bodies, save our souls, direct our thoughts,
and bring us safe to the heavenly country, our eternal
        home,
    where Father, Son and Holy Spirit ever reign,
    one God for ever and ever. *Amen.*

44. *The Powers that Be*

Our Lord lays down a spiritual principle
Render to Caesar the things that are Caesar's,
and to God the things that are God's.

S. Mark 12: 17

St Paul and St Peter teach a duty to the state
Let every person be subject to the governing authorities.

Romans 13: 1

Be subject for the Lord's sake to every human institution,
whether it be to the emperor as supreme, or to
governors as sent by him to punish those who do wrong
and to praise those who do right.

Live as free men, yet without using your freedom as a
pretext for evil; but live as servants of God. Honor all
men. Love the brotherhood. Fear God. Honor the
emperor.

I Peter 2: 13-17

Guidance when duties conflict
Peter and John answered them, Whether it is right in
the sight of God to listen to you rather than to God,
you must judge; for we cannot but speak of what we
have seen and heard. . . .

Peter and the apostles answered, We must obey God
rather than men.

Acts 4: 19, 20; 5: 29

Let us remember before God:
our duty to our Government in all things lawful;
our opportunity to witness to the power of the Christian
faith by the quality of our citizenship.

182. GRANT US, O GOD, a vision of our land, fair as she
      might be:
     a land of justice, where none shall prey on others;
     a land of plenty, where poverty shall cease to fester;
     a land of brotherhood, where success shall be founded
       on service, and honour be given to worth alone;
     a land of peace, where order shall not rest on force,
       but on the love of all for their land,
         the great mother of the common life and welfare.

183. O FATHER OF JUSTICE, of thine infinite goodness
     direct the hearts of all who bear authority. Help
     them with the power of thy Holy Spirit; protect
     them from the snares of the enemy and the pride
     of power; and grant that rulers and people may
     with one mind serve thee our God and King,
     through Jesus Christ.

184. WHERE THE MIND is without fear and the head is
      held high;
        where knowledge is free;
     where the world has not been broken up into
        fragments
        by narrow domestic walls;
     where words come out from the depth of truth;
     where tireless striving stretches its arms towards
        perfection;
     where the clear stream of reason has not lost its way
      into the dreary desert sand of dead habit;
     where the mind is led forward by thee
      into ever-widening thought and action—
     Into that heaven of freedom, my Father, let my
        country awake.

117

45. *Christ in Industry*

Is not this the carpenter?

S. Mark 6: 3

Who serves as a soldier at his own expense? Who plants a vineyard without eating any of its fruit? Who tends a flock without getting some of the milk?
Do I say this on human authority? Does not the law say the same? For it is written in the law of Moses,
> You shall not muzzle an ox when it is treading out the grain.

Is it for oxen that God is concerned? Does he not speak entirely for our sake? It was written for our sake, because the plowman should plow in hope and the thresher thresh in hope of a share in the crop.

I Corinthians 9: 7-10

I rejoice in the Lord greatly that now at length you have revived your concern for me. . . . Not that I complain of want; for I have learned, in whatever state I am, to be content.

Philippians 4: 10-11

Let us recall with penitence the small part the Church in the West has taken in the social and industrial changes of the last two hundred years, and the weak impact which the Church makes upon the industrial world today.
Let us thank God for the prophets and reformers who have revealed spiritual issues and struggled to improve conditions and for dedicated people in industry today, who strive for right relationships, true values and just conditions.
Remembering the rapid growth in industry which is taking place all over the world, and especially in Asia and Africa, let us pray for a spirit of service to the community in all involved in ownership, management and labour;

for a deeper valuation of human relationships in industry,
and a new realization of the importance of family life;

for Christians in industry, that through them the justice
and love of God may find entry into industrial concerns;

for God's blessing on experiments in partnership, profit-
sharing, and planning to meet difficulties;

for God's blessing on pastoral and evangelistic experiments,
especially on industrial chaplains, and priest-workmen.

May Christ be acknowledged as the Lord of all life!

The Lord's Prayer

185.   O LORD OUR GOD, King of Life,
        as we take our place in the working-day world,
            with its cares and labours,
            with its temptations,
        help us to serve thee in all that we do.
        Lead us in the right path.
        Grant us to walk in safety.
        Teach us to do what is for our salvation.
    In the name of Jesus, thy Son, our Lord and Saviour.

186.   JESUS, THE MASTER CARPENTER, who at the last
        through wood and nails, purchased man's whole
        salvation; wield well thy tools in this workshop of
        thine, that we who come rough-hewn may here be
        fashioned to a truer beauty by thy hand.

187.   O LORD, make thy way plain before us;
            let thy glory be our end;
                thy word our rule;
            and as always, thy will be done.   *Amen.*

46. Nations United

The vision of the prophets reflects the desire of the people of all nations

It shall come to pass in the latter days that the mountain of the house of the Lord shall be established as the highest of the mountains, and shall be raised up above the hills; and peoples shall flow to it, and many nations shall come, and say:

> Come, let us go up to the mountain of the Lord, to the house of the God of Jacob; that he may teach us his ways and we may walk in his paths.

For out of Zion shall go forth the law, and the word of the Lord from Jerusalem. He shall judge between many peoples, and shall decide for strong nations afar off; and they shall beat their swords into plowshares, and their spears into pruning hooks;

nation shall not lift up sword against nation, neither shall they learn war any more.

Micah 4: 1-3

The wilderness and the solitary place shall be glad; and the desert shall rejoice, and blossom as the rose . . .

Then the eyes of the blind shall be opened, and the ears of the deaf shall be unstopped.

Then shall the lame man leap as an hart, and the tongue of the dumb shall sing: for in the wilderness shall waters break out, and streams in the desert.

Isaiah 35: 1, 5, 6 (R.V.)

Thus says the Lord of hosts:

> Old men and old women shall again sit in the streets of Jerusalem, each with staff in hand for very age. And the streets of the city shall be full of boys and girls playing in its streets.

Zechariah 8: 4, 5

Let us thank God:

that the leaders of the nations now meet together round the conference table to deal with problems of world peace, to correct injustices and to discuss grievances;

for the growing recognition of a common standard of human rights and freedom for all peoples and all nations;

for the sharing of knowledge and art and culture, for the mutual inspiration and example in education by means of the United Nations Educational, Scientific and Cultural Organization;

for the sharing of medical science, the rescue work in emergency and epidemic, the efforts to banish widespread disease, undertaken by the World Health Organization;

for the joint consultation in the Food and Agriculture Organization in its efforts to preserve the fertility of the earth, fight pests, increase food production and distribute supplies more equally;

for the care for homeless refugees and the relief for warstricken people, given through the United Nations Refugee Emergency Fund.

Let us pray:

for all the national representatives in the United Nations Organization, that they may be guided aright in seeing and working for the things that belong unto peace;

for the nations and their leaders, that they may be ready to make the sacrifices necessary to achieve a family of nations living together in peace and prosperity;

for the guidance and blessing of the Holy Spirit on the Commission of the Churches on International Affairs, in its relations with the United Nations Organization and in its national commissions.

Let us remember that the weaknesses seen in the working of
the United Nations Organization are those of human
nature; that only when God is acknowledged as Lord
of all will men's visions of a new world be fulfilled.

The Lord's Prayer

188.   ALMIGHTY GOD, OUR HEAVENLY FATHER,
            guide we beseech thee the nations of the world
                into the way of justice and truth
            and establish among them that peace
                which is the fruit of righteousness.

189.   O HEAVENLY FATHER, we thank thee for those who
        out of the bitter memories of strife and loss
                are seeking a more excellent way
                for the nations of the world,
            whereby justice and order may be maintained
            and the differences of peoples be resolved in equity.
        We pray thee to establish their purpose on sure
                foundations
                and to prosper their labours, that thy will
                may be done;
            for the sake of Jesus Christ our Lord.

190.   O ALMIGHTY GOD, who alone canst order the unruly
            wills and affections of sinful men: Grant unto the
            nations of the world that they may come to love
            that which thou commandest and so obtain that
            which thou dost promise; through Jesus Christ
            our Lord.

191.   ALL THE ENDS of the earth shall remember and turn
            unto the Lord, and all the kindreds of the nations
            shall worship before thee. For the kingdom is the
            Lord's: and he is the ruler over the nations.   *Amen.*

47. *The Christian Home*

The child Jesus at Nazareth

And the child grew and became strong, filled with wisdom; and the favor of God was upon him. . . .

And he went down with them [Mary and Joseph] and came to Nazareth, and was obedient to them; . . .

S. Luke 2: 40, 51

Jesus speaks of the divine institution of marriage

. . . From the beginning of creation, God made them male and female. For this reason a man shall leave his father and mother and be joined to his wife, and the two shall become one . . .

What therefore God has joined together, let not man put asunder.

S. Mark 10: 6-9

A whole family is baptized

One who heard us was a woman named Lydia, from the city of Thyatira, a seller of purple goods, who was a worshiper of God. The Lord opened her heart to give heed to what was said by Paul.

And when she was baptized, with her household, she besought us, saying, If you have judged me to be faithful to the Lord, come to my house and stay.

Acts 16: 14, 15

Paul greets a Christian household

Paul, a prisoner for Christ Jesus, and Timothy our brother, To Philemon our beloved fellow worker and Apphia our sister and Archippus our fellow soldier, and the church in your house:

Grace to you and peace from God our Father and the Lord Jesus Christ.

Philemon: 1-3

Let us thank God:

> for the divine institution of family life with its mutual love and caring, its joy and support in trouble;
>
> that our Lord Jesus Christ shared the life of an earthly home, was obedient to Mary and Joseph, was ready to leave his home at God's call, and when dying on the cross made provision for his mother;
>
> for all that Christ and his Church mean to us in our family life;
>
> for the witness to others of the Christian home.

Let us pray:

> that God's plan of family life may be understood and accepted in all parts of the world;
>
> that there may be a return in the West to Christian standards of faithfulness in marriage;
>
> that in other parts polygamy may be abandoned and a deep spiritual and lifelong ideal of marriage be accepted;
>
> for broken homes, that the love of God may redeem and re-make;
>
> for the Refugee Service of the World Council of Churches and for all who are seeking to help the homeless.

The Lord's Prayer

192. LORD GOD ALMIGHTY, FATHER OF EVERY FAMILY, against whom no door can be shut:

> Enter all homes, we beseech thee, with the angel of thy presence, to hallow them in pureness and beauty of love;
>
> and by thy dear Son, born in a stable, move our hearts to hear the cry of the homeless, and to convert all sordid and bitter dwellings into households of thine;
>
> through Jesus Christ our Lord.

193. O God our Father, in whom all the families of the earth are blessed: We pray thee to regard with thy loving-kindness the homes of our country; that marriage may be held in due honour by the Church, by the State, and by society; and that husbands and wives may live faithfully together, in honour preferring one another. We pray that the members of every family may be rich in mutual understanding and forbearance, in courtesy and kindness, bearing one another's burdens, and so fulfilling the law of Christ, thy Son, our Lord.

194. Heavenly Father,
from whom all fatherhood in heaven and earth is named:
  Bless, we beseech thee, all children,
    and give to their parents,
    and to all in whose charge they may be,
      thy spirit of wisdom and love;
  so that the home in which they grow up
  may be to them an image of thy kingdom,
and the care of their parents a likeness of thy love.

195. O Lord Jesus Christ, who on the cross didst remember
  thy Mother and thy friend,
  make our homes to be homes of love.
Spread thy grace over every relationship of human life,
  so that all our earthly love
  may be gathered up into the love of God,
  and thy kingdom made manifest to men
  in the homes of thy people.

196. We bow our knees unto the Father,
from whom every family in heaven and in earth is named.

48. *The Kingdom of His Christ*

In the Kingdom of God uncompromising obedience to God is essential
Again, the devil took him to a very high mountain, and
showed him all the kingdoms of the world and the
glory of them; and he said to him,
All these I will give you, if you will fall down and
worship me.
Then Jesus said to him,
Begone, Satan! for it is written, You shall worship
the Lord your God and him only shall you serve.

S. Matthew 4: 8-10

Spiritual principles are more important than material things
Seek first his kingdom and his righteousness, and all these
things shall be yours as well. *S. Matthew 6: 33*

Humble service is the highest qualification
Whoever would be great among you must be your servant
and whoever would be first among you must be slave
of all. *S. Mark 10: 44*

Let us pray that God may bless and uphold our brethren
in Communist countries today, keeping them faithful, and
accepting their witness.

OUR FATHER . . .

197.   O GOD, THE KING OF RIGHTEOUSNESS, lead us,
we pray thee,
in ways of justice and peace:
inspire us to break down all tyranny and
oppression,
to gain for every man his due reward,
and from every man his due service;
that each may live for all and all may care for each,
in Jesus Christ our Lord.

198. O GOD OF JUSTICE AND LOVE, forgive us and our forefathers that we have been so lukewarm in working for thy kingdom. Forgive thy Church in that the dispossessed of all nations have not seen in it the hope of a new order and the promise of human brotherhood and world peace.

Cleanse and renew us, and teach us to put thy kingdom before every other loyalty and thy will before every desire, through Jesus Christ our Lord.

199. O THOU WHO ART THE LIGHT of the world,
the desire of all nations,
and the shepherd of our souls:
let thy light shine in the darkness,
and by the lifting up of thy cross
gather the peoples unto thee,
that all the ends of the earth may see
the salvation of God.

200. O CHRIST, who in thyself art both the gospel and the kingdom,
show us how to preach good news
to those who fight for the kingdom of this world.
Help us to proclaim thy love for them
and call them in to work for the new heaven and earth
which comes down from heaven,
so that both they and we may rejoice in thy kingdom
of righteousness, peace and joy, which has no end,
and worship the God who never fails,
even our Creator and Saviour, blessed for evermore.

Amen.

49. *The Christian Warfare*

St Paul shows us the character of our warfare

Though we live in the world we are not carrying on a worldly war, for the weapons of our warfare are not worldly but have divine power to destroy strongholds. We destroy arguments and every proud obstacle to the knowledge of God, and take every thought captive to obey Christ.

II Corinthians 10: 3-5

He enumerates our spiritual weapons

Finally, be strong in the Lord and in the strength of his might. Put on the whole armor of God, that you may be able to stand against the wiles of the devil.

For we are not contending against flesh and blood, but against the principalities, against the powers, against the world rulers of this present darkness, against the spiritual hosts of wickedness in the heavenly places.

Therefore take the whole armor of God, that you may be able to withstand in the evil day, and having done all, to stand.

Stand therefore, having girded your loins with truth, and having put on the breastplate of righteousness, and having shod your feet with the equipment of the gospel of peace; above all taking the shield of faith, with which you can quench all the flaming darts of the evil one.

Ephesians 6: 10-16

Meditation

Let us remember our Lord healing an enemy at his arrest, mocked in the guardroom yet undefeated in love, on the cross praying for those who nailed him there.

Let us meditate on the only weapons Christians may use, praying that evil may never defeat us into retaliation, but that we may overcome evil with good, and win men by love and truth.

128

201. O LORD GOD, keep ever in our remembrance
the life and death of our Saviour Jesus Christ.
Make the thought of his love powerful to win us from
evil.
As he toiled and sorrowed and suffered for us,
in fighting against sin,
so may we endure constantly and labour diligently,
as his soldiers and servants,
looking ever unto him
and counting it all joy to be partakers with him
in his conflict, his cross and his victory.

202. ETERNAL GOD, in whose perfect kingdom
no sword is drawn but the sword of righteousness,
and no strength known but the strength of love:
help thy soldiers to fight the good fight of faith,
refusing the weapons of the devil and the world,
and overcoming hatred with love, evil with
goodness, falsehood with truth,
and so extending the victory of the cross;
through him who triumphed thereon,
even thy Son, our Saviour Jesus Christ.

203. LORD JESUS, who wast silent when men nailed thee
to the cross, and by pain didst triumph over pain:
Pour thy spirit, we beseech thee, on thy servants
when they suffer, that in their quietness and
courage thou mayest triumph again; who livest
and reignest in the glory of the eternal Trinity,
God, world without end.

The Lord's Prayer

204. THE PEACE OF GOD
which passeth all understanding
guard our hearts and thoughts
in Christ Jesus. *Amen.*

129

VIII. THE ENDS OF THE EARTH

50. A Light to the Nations

The first worshippers from the nations

Now when Jesus was born in Bethlehem of Judea in the
days of Herod the king, behold, wise men from the
East came to Jerusalem, saying,
Where is he who has been born king of the Jews?
For we have seen his star in the East, and have
come to worship him. . . .

and going into the house they saw the child with Mary
his mother, and they fell down and worshiped him.
Then, opening their treasures, they offered him gifts,
gold and frankincense and myrrh.   *S. Matthew 2: 1, 2, 11*

St Paul sees that salvation is for all nations

The mystery was made known to me by revelation . . .
that is, how the Gentiles are fellow-heirs, members of
the same body, and partakers of the promise in Christ
Jesus through the gospel. . . .

To me, though I am the very least of all the saints, this
grace was given, to preach to the Gentiles the unsearchable riches of Christ.   *Ephesians 3: 3, 6, 8*

In the worship of the wise men let us see the promise that
all nations shall come and worship thee, O Lord.

In the founding of the Church in every land let us see the
fulfilment of the promise of the Epiphany.

205. ALMIGHTY AND EVERLASTING GOD, the brightness of faithful souls, who didst bring the Gentiles to thy light and make known unto them him who is the true light, and the bright and morning star:

Fill, we beseech thee, the world with thy glory, and show thyself by the radiance of thy light unto all nations; through Jesus Christ our Lord.

206. LORD JESUS CHRIST, who in the offerings of the wise men didst receive an earnest of the worship of the nations:

Grant that thy Church may never cease to proclaim the good news of thy love, that all men may come to worship thee as their Saviour and King, who livest and reignest world without end.

207. LORD OF THE HARVEST, the nations are waiting for thy message, and asking for messengers, and there are few who go, and few who give, and few who pray.

O grant that we may hear thy voice, and help in whatever way we can, by prayer, by gifts, and by service, to make thy gospel known to all the world; for the sake of Jesus Christ our Saviour.

The Lord's Prayer

208. GOD BE MERCIFUL unto us, and bless us, and shew us the light of his countenance, and be merciful unto us;

that thy way may be known upon earth, thy saving health among all nations . . .

Let the people praise thee, O God; yea, let all the people praise thee.

Then shall the earth bring forth her increase, and God, even our own God, shall give us his blessing.

The Light of the World is also the Light of Asia
  Again Jesus spoke to them, saying,

> I am the light of the world; he who follows me will not
> walk in darkness, but will have the light of life. . . .
> If you continue in my word, you are truly my disciples,
> . . . and you will know the truth, and the truth will
> make you free. . . . So if the Son makes you free, you
> will be free indeed.

S. John 8: 12, 31, 32, 36

St Paul's gratitude for one of the Asian Churches
  We always thank God, the Father of our Lord Jesus
  Christ, when we pray for you, because we have heard
  of your faith in Christ Jesus and of the love which you
  have for all the saints, because of the hope laid up for
  you in heaven.
  Of this you have heard before in the word of the truth,
  the gospel which has come to you, as indeed in the
  whole world it is bearing fruit and growing—so among
  yourselves, from the day you heard and understood
  the grace of God in truth.

Colossians 1: 3-6

Let us pray:
  for the nations in Asia in their newly-won independence,
    that each may build its national life on justice, peace
    and unity;
  for our Christian brethren in Asia, that through their
    thinking and living they may show forth the truth and
    love of Christ to their fellow-countrymen.

209. GRANT THY SERVANTS, O GOD, to be set on fire with
      thy spirit, strengthened by thy power, illumined
      by thy splendour, filled with thy grace, and to go
      forward by thine aid.

Let us thank God:

for the Church in Asia, planted in apostolic times, ever finding new life after each era of darkness or persecution;

for the readiness of Christians in Asia to suffer for their faith;

for their insights into the gospel and their witness to the power of Christ in their lives;

for their insistence on the need of unity in Christ's Church.

Let us join in prayers offered by Asian Christians, praying with them for their countries and for our own.

A prayer for India

210. WE INTERCEDE BEFORE THEE for beloved Hindustan
and our prayer is the same
as that of ancient seekers after thee,
' From darkness lead us to light
and from shadows to reality'.
Mercifully grant that millions of this land
forever engaged in arduous pilgrimages
in search of peace and satisfaction
may at last lay down their weary burdens
at the feet of him who gives rest and peace
to all those who labour and are heavy laden.
May they come at last to the haven of peace,
even Jesus Christ,
and find in him thine own response
to their age-long quest.
To that end the frankincense of India's meditation,
the myrrh of its renunciation and sacrifice,
and the gold of its devotion
be laid at the feet of Jesus Christ
and may he be crowned Lord of all.

Augustine Ralla Ram

A prayer for Japan

211. WE BESEECH THEE, O GOD ALMIGHTY, that thou grant us the power to do thy will and to be of service to thy holy purpose, preparing the way to build up thy kingdom here in the Orient.

Let us learn to do everything for the ministry of reconciliation and redemption, to heal the wounded souls and to restore the broken hearts, that we may strengthen the ties of the Christian fellowship between the nations of the world.

We lift our hearts to thee, O God our Lord, in the genuine desire to share each other's burdens with our fellow Christians of every nation. In the name of our Saviour Jesus Christ, our Lord.

Akira Ebisawa

A prayer for China

212. WE PRAISE THEE, OUR FATHER, that even in the hour of darkness we can come to thee with confidence and unflinching faith.

We know that thou art the ruler of nations and the maker of history; we know that nothing that men can do can ever frustrate thy holy and righteous will; we know that thou canst make even the wrath of men to praise thee.

Help us, Father, to learn the lessons that have come out of conflict; help us to work for the new day that will bring us one step nearer thy kingdom.

Dear Lord and Father of mankind, grant that the day may not be too far off when the nations will become one, when war will be abolished, and when we shall all live peacefully together as brethren in thy holy family.

A Chinese Christian

Let us say the Lord's Prayer with loving intention for our Christian brethren in China.

52. Africa

The first recorded African conversion

Then Philip opened his mouth, and beginning with this
scripture he told the Ethiopian eunuch the good news
of Jesus.

And as they went along the road they came to some water,
and the eunuch said, See, here is water. What is to
prevent my being baptized?

And he commanded the chariot to stop, and they both
went down into the water, Philip and the eunuch, and
he baptized him.

And when they came up out of the water, the Spirit
of the Lord caught up Philip; and the eunuch saw him
no more, and went on his way rejoicing.

Acts 8: 35-39

There are no racial divisions in Christ's new creation

For he is our peace, who has made us both one, and has
broken down the dividing wall of hostility, by abolish-
ing in his flesh the law of commandments and ordinances, that he might create in himself one new man in
place of the two, so making peace, and might reconcile
us both to God in one body through the cross, thereby
bringing the hostility to an end.

Ephesians 2: 14-16

St Paul's thanksgiving for Christians young in the faith

We give thanks to God always for you all, constantly
mentioning you in our prayers, remembering before
our God and Father your work of faith and labor of
love and steadfastness of hope in our Lord Jesus Christ.

For we know, brethren beloved by God, that he has
chosen you; for our gospel came to you not only in
word, but also in power and in the Holy Spirit and
with full conviction.

I Thessalonians 1: 2-5

Let us ask God's forgiveness:

for the many grievous sins inflicted upon Africa—the slave trade, forced labour, the drink traffic;

for racial prejudice and hatred in white people and in black also;

for commercial exploitation by peoples of Europe and Asia.

Let us thank God:

for the great African Christians of early centuries, especially St Augustine of Hippo;

for the Church of Christ today, bringing good news of deliverance from fear, and for racial brotherhood in Christ;

for many who have loved the African people—government servants, teachers and missionaries, settlers and traders;

for peacemakers who try to right the wrongs and to understand the difficulties of other races;

for Christians in Kenya, who are ready to face death rather than indulge in racial hatred;

for the fellowship of African Christians—their joy in worship, their capacity for suffering, their clear and simple faith, their happy laughter.

Let us pray:

for Africans whose tribal life has been broken up by contact with Western industrial conditions;

for Christian Africans tempted to join in racial hatred and retaliation;

for all governments in Africa, whether independent or trustee, that they may fulfil their responsibilities to all their peoples;

for all who go to serve in Africa in any capacity.

Let us worship with a Xhosa Christian

213.   THOU ART THE GREAT GOD—he who is in heaven.
    Thou art the Creator of life, thou makest
        the regions above.
    Thou art the Hunter who hunts for souls.
    Thou art the Leader who goes before us.
    Thou art the great Mantle which covers us.
    Thou art he whose hands are with wounds.
    Thou art he whose feet are with wounds.
    Thou art he whose blood is a trickling stream.
    Thou art he whose blood was spilled for us.

Let us pray with a Bantu pastor

214.   WE OFFER OUR THANKS TO THEE
      for sending thy only Son to die for us all.
    In a world suffocated with colour bars,
      how sweet a thing it is to know
    that in thee we all belong to one family.
      There are times when we,
      unprivileged people,
    weep tears that are not loud but deep,
    when we think of the suffering we experience.
    We come to thee, our only hope and refuge.
    Help us, O God, to refuse to be embittered
      against those who handle us with harshness.
      We are grateful to thee
    for the gift of laughter at all times.
    Save us from hatred of those who oppress us.
    May we follow the spirit of thy Son Jesus Christ.

The Lord's Prayer

215.   O THOU, who art the Lion of Judah,
    be thou also the Lion of Africa,
      and burst all the chains
    that still bind our African brothers,
    and deliver them from all fear.   *Amen.*

53. Europe

St Paul's thanksgiving for the first Church in Europe

I thank my God in all my remembrance of you, always in every prayer of mine for you all making my prayer with joy, thankful for your partnership in the gospel from the first day until now. And I am sure that he who began a good work in you will bring it to completion at the day of Jesus Christ.

Philippians 1 : 3-6

Warning against materialism and pride

For you say, I am rich, I have prospered, and I need nothing; not knowing that you are wretched, pitiable, poor, blind, and naked.

Therefore I counsel you to buy from me gold refined by fire, that you may be rich, and white garments to clothe you and to keep the shame of your nakedness from being seen, and salve to anoint your eyes, that you may see.

Revelation 3 : 17-18

The strongest force in the world

Not by might, nor by power, but by my Spirit, says the Lord of hosts.

Zechariah 4 : 6

Let us thank God:

for missionaries all down the ages who have gone out from the Churches in Europe to proclaim the Gospel of Christ;

for the new life in the Churches of Europe after the war;

for the numberless faithful Christians who pray and give for Christ's mission to the world;

for many in Europe today who suffer for Christ's sake, believing the promise that those who are faithful unto death shall receive the crown of life.

For a return to the Christian faith

216.   LORD, as we stand before thee,
            we know that we are not worthy
            to be called thy servants.
    We have not given our whole life to thee
        and we have served other masters besides thee.
    Our faith is weak and we have been afraid
            to confess it before our fellows.
    We have not taken thy promises seriously
            and have not believed
        that thy Word has power to save man.
    But, Lord, we cannot live without thee.
    And as we hear thee calling us again today,
        we would not harden our hearts.
            Allow us to return to thee,
        forgive us for our halfheartedness
            and help thou our unbelief,
    so that we may learn to live as thy children,
        to serve thee with all our heart
        and to be thy witnesses unto man.

For the cleansing and strengthening of the Church

217.   MOST GRACIOUS FATHER, we humbly beseech thee
            for thy Holy Catholic Church.
            Fill it with all truth;
            in all truth with all peace.
        Where it is corrupt, purge it;
        where it is in error, direct it;   .
        where anything is amiss, reform it;
    where it is right, strengthen and confirm it;
        where it is in want, furnish it;
        where it is divided and rent asunder,
        ·   make up the breaches of it,
            O thou Holy One of Israel.

218. ALMIGHTY GOD, FATHER, SON AND HOLY GHOST,
       we praise thee, we thank thee,
       that thou hast founded thy kingdom
           in this world of death,
       that thy Word is still proclaimed
       and that thou gatherest thy people.
  Give thy Church, through thy grace,
       courage fearlessly to confess its faith
       and thankfully to bear witness to thy holy love,
           and keep us in the right path,
               that amidst all enmity
       we neither let ourselves be driven to despair
       nor think too highly of ourselves.
  Console those who suffer for the sake of thy gospel.
       Abide with those who are imprisoned.
       Strengthen them with the power
           of thy life-giving Word
       and keep us from weakness and despair.
       Deliver us from our distress and need!

219. ALMIGHTY AND EVERLASTING GOD,
  who hast revealed thy glory in Christ
           among all nations:
       Preserve the works of thy mercy
           that thy Church,
       which is spread throughout the world,
       may persevere with steadfast faith
       in the confession of thy name:
       through Jesus Christ our Lord. *Amen.*

54. North America

A new country

Now the Lord said to Abram,

Go from your country and your kindred and your father's house to the land that I will show you.

And I will make of you a great nation, and I will bless you, and make your name great, so that you will be a blessing . . . by you all the families of the earth will bless themselves.

Genesis 12: 1-3

The dedication of wealth

Her merchandise and her hire will be dedicated to the Lord; it will not be stored or hoarded, but her merchandise will supply abundant food and fine clothing for those who dwell before the Lord.

Isaiah 23: 18

Values in life

A man's life does not consist in the abundance of his possessions.

S. Luke 12: 15

Man does not live by bread alone, but . . . by everything that proceeds out of the mouth of the Lord.

Deuteronomy 8: 3

The responsibility of stewardship

To whom much is given, of him will
much be required.

S. Luke 12: 48

Let us thank God:

for the generous share of North America in the missionary work of the Church Universal;

for the outpouring of gifts in compassion for the world's need.

Let us pray:

> for a deeper realization of our Lord's warning that from
> those to whom much is given much will be required;
> for humility and faithfulness in face of misrepresentation;
> for ever-deepening purity of motive.

The Lord's Prayer

Let us join with an American Christian as he prays for his country

220. ETERNAL GOD, FATHER OF ALL NATIONS, we praise
thee for the brotherhood of many races and peoples
that exists among us. From the ends of the earth
thou hast brought to our land the children of many
nations. Help us more worthily to blend them into
one family, and to make of them one people whose
God is the Lord.

> Enlarge our sympathies, widen the expanse of our
> generosity, give us the eyes of Christ that we may
> see all men and women as our kindred.

> Especially grant thy blessing on our churches, that
> they may become in deed and truth members of
> the one, universal Church of Christ, and may be so
> guided by thy providence and nourished by thy
> grace, that they may minister to the whole world's
> good, to the glory of thy Son, our Lord and
> Saviour.

And with a Canadian Christian

221. O LORD, remember the lonely who dwell upon our
frontiers, the folk of the plains and the mountains,
the fishermen and their families, the miners and
the lumbermen, in all our fair provinces.

> Grant us as a people to attain to unity amid all the
> rich diversity of many national origins that make
> up our Dominion.

> Blend us into one family under thy divine fatherhood
> revealed in Jesus Christ.

142

222. O GOD, who hast made the earth so varied and cast
the races of men in so many different moulds,

we who dwell in these lovely islands of the western
sea, pray for all thy children.

Grant that through the power of Jesus Christ we may
be freed from such spiritual shackles as still
enslave us, that in his light all darkness of super-
stition may be dispelled, and that we may enter
into the full, joyous life of thy kingdom.

Bless all who teach us in school or college, all who
seek to deliver us from sickness or poverty; but
especially all who strive to bring us and keep us
under the influence of Christ.

May the Church in these islands grow ever purer
and stronger, that through it thou mayest be
glorified in the lives of all its members: through
Jesus Christ our Lord.

Finally, let us worship with an Eskimo Christian

223. TO THEE THE GOD OF TRUTH, of light and of love,
who art highest and noblest,
we bring our worship.

Cause us to hate that which thou dost hate,
and to love that which thou dost love,
that we may be thy true children
today and always. *Amen.*

55. *Latin America*

Religious freedom is an urgent issue today

> John said to him, Teacher, we saw a man casting out demons in your name, and we forbade him, because he was not following us.

> But Jesus said, Do not forbid him; for no one who does a mighty work in my name will be able soon after to speak evil of me. For he that is not against us is for us.

S. Mark 9 : 38-40

The Statue of Christ in the Andes is a pledge of peace between two nations

> How beautiful upon the mountains are the feet of him who brings good tidings, who publishes peace, who brings good tidings of good, who publishes salvation, who says to Zion, Your God reigns. . . .

> The Lord has bared his holy arm before the eyes of all the nations; and all the ends of the earth shall see the salvation of our God.

Isaiah 52: 7, 10

Pentecostalist groups have shown a great example in evangelism

> The fruit of the Spirit is love, joy, peace, long-suffering, kindness, goodness, faithfulness, meekness, temperance; against such there is no law.

Galatians 5: 22-23

Let us pray:

> for a spirit of toleration and brotherhood among all Christians;

> for a spirit of charity and forgiveness in all whose religious liberty is limited or threatened,
>> that the love of Christ may fill their hearts, free them from all resentment and bitterness and sustain them in all persecution;

> for a change of heart in governments and officials who use their power for religious repression.

The Lord's Prayer

144

For all who suffer for their faith

224.   O LORD who hast promised a blessing for all who
suffer for righteousness' sake: Grant to all our
brethren persecuted for the truth that they may
rejoice in being counted worthy to suffer dishonour
for thy name.

Strengthen their faith and renew their love, that in
their patience they may possess their souls and
win their persecutors to penitence and new
brotherhood in thee, for the sake of him who
suffered shame and reproach and remained
invincible in his love, even thy redeeming Son,
Christ our Lord.

For the Holy Spirit's power

225.   O GOD, who in the exaltation of thy Son Jesus Christ
dost sanctify thy universal Church:
Shed abroad in every race and nation
the gift of his spirit;
that the work wrought by his power
at the first preaching of the gospel
may be extended throughout the whole world.

For the nations

226.   O GOD, OUR FATHER, give to the nations of the world
a new heart of comradeship; that every people
may bring its tribute of excellence to the common
treasury, and all the world may go forward in the
new and living way which he hath consecrated
for us, who now liveth and reigneth, with thee and
the spirit of truth, one God, world without end.

INTO THE FAITHFUL HANDS OF OUR GOD
we commit ourselves and our brethren
now and always.   *Amen.*

56. South-West Pacific

God's salvation shall spread to the ends of the earth

Turn to me and be saved, all the ends of the earth! For I am God, and there is no other. By myself I have sworn, from my mouth has gone forth in righteousness a word that shall not return: To me every knee shall bow, every tongue shall swear.

Isaiah 45: 22-23

The Lord God is a shepherd to his people

As a shepherd seeks out his flock when some of his sheep have been scattered abroad, so will I seek out my sheep; and I will rescue them from all places where they have been scattered on a day of clouds and thick darkness. . . . On fat pasture they shall feed on the mountains of Israel.

I myself will be the shepherd of my sheep.

Ezekiel 34: 12, 14, 15

A warning not to forget God

And you shall eat and be full, and you shall bless the Lord your God for the good land he has given you.

Take heed lest you forget the Lord your God, by not keeping his commandments and his ordinances and his statutes, which I command you this day: lest, when you have eaten and are full, and have built goodly houses and live in them, and when your herds and flocks multiply, and your silver and gold is multiplied, and all that you have is multiplied, then your heart be lifted up, and you forget the Lord your God. . . .

Beware lest you say in your heart, My power and the might of my hand have gotten me this wealth.

Deuteronomy 8: 10-14, 17

The Lord's Prayer

Prayer of a New Zealand Christian

227. O ETERNAL FATHER, whose love is boundless
  and whose kingdom has penetrated
  to the uttermost part of the earth,
 we thank thee
  that the light of thy everlasting gospel
  has dawned in the islands of the Southern Seas.
 We thank thee that thou didst raise up
   and inspire men and women
  to leave the comforts of their native countries
   to be Light-bearers
  in the darkest corners of the earth
  and to spread the knowledge of thyself
  and thy Son Jesus Christ.
 We thank thee for the fellowship
  of many races in thy Church
  who join in seeking the fulfilment
  of the vision of a world won for thee
 through thy blessed Son Jesus Christ our Lord.

For the Islands of the Pacific

228. ALMIGHTY GOD, for whom the isles do wait,
  we pray that the Church in the islands of the Pacific
   may be strengthened to meet the difficulties arising
   from immense distances.
  Send down thy blessing, we pray thee, on the peoples
   of the islands; upon medical and other workers;
   upon those on missionary vessels; and upon all
   who teach or are taught in the schools.
  Guide them, O Lord, in every difficulty;
   protect them in every danger;
   strengthen them in every temptation;
   and gladden them with the sense of thy presence;
  through Jesus Christ our Lord.

229.   O LOVING FATHER,
     from this fair land under southern skies
         we lift up our hearts in praise to thee
         for thy great goodness to us as a people;
     for those brave souls who, sailing unknown seas,
     found here a wealth of beauty and of opportunity;
     for those stout-hearted pioneers who, undaunted
         by difficulties and defeats, crossed the ranges,
         and in this land of wide horizons,
             built their homes and laid the foundations
                 of a new order of life.
     We confess with shame
         our absorption in material things,
         our love of pleasure,
         our lust for gain,
         our failure to use aright
             the rich resources of our land
         and our slowness to fulfil
             our missionary duty.
     Forgive us, O Lord, and grant us the vision
         of thy high purpose for this nation
         and of thy saving love for all mankind,
             through Jesus Christ our Lord.

230.   BLESSED BE THE LORD GOD,
     who only doeth wondrous things;
     and blessed be the Name of his Majesty
                 for ever:
     and all the earth shall be filled
                 with his Majesty.
                 Amen. Amen.

IX. WINNING THE WORLD

57. Fear not, little flock

Fear not, little flock, for it is your Father's good pleasure
   to give you the kingdom.

S. Luke 12: 32

The seventy returned with joy, saying,
   Lord, even the demons are subject to us in your name!
And he said to them,
   I saw Satan fall like lightning from heaven.
   Behold, I have given you authority to tread upon
serpents and scorpions, and over all the power of the
enemy; and nothing shall hurt you.
   Nevertheless do not rejoice in this, that the spirits
are subject to you; but rejoice that your names are
written in heaven.

S. Luke 10: 17-20

For consider your call, brethren; not many of you were
   wise according to worldly standards, not many were
   powerful, not many were of noble birth;
but God chose what is foolish in the world to shame the
   wise, God chose what is weak in the world to shame the
   strong, God chose what is low and despised in the world,
   even things that are not, to bring to nothing things that
   are, so that no human being might boast in the presence
   of God.

I Corinthians 1: 26-29

Let us thank God:
> for the sure confidence of his promises
> for our unshakable trust in his calling
> for his never-failing presence within his Church

Let us pray:
> for the Church in lands where Christians are a small
> minority;
> for the small groups of Christians in countries where
> Christ may not be openly proclaimed;
> for Christians living in areas of particular difficulty,
> that they may be brave in their witness and Christ-
> like in their lives;
> that we may be faithful in our prayers for them.

The Lord's Prayer

231. GRANT UNTO US, O GOD,
> that we may never be ashamed to confess
> the faith of Christ crucified,
> but may manfully fight under his banner
> against sin, the world, and the devil,
> and continue Christ's faithful soldiers and servants
> unto our lives' end.

232. WE BESEECH THEE, O LORD, for all members of thy
Holy Catholic Church throughout the world, that
they may ever remember that, wheresoever there
be a congregation of the faithful, there the Lord
of the Church is in the midst.

233. REMEMBER, O LORD, what thou hast wrought in us,
> and not what we deserve,
> and as thou has called us to thy service,
> make us worthy of our calling;
> through Jesus Christ our Lord.

234.　O HOLY SPIRIT,
　　　　grant us, we pray thee, the gift of courage.
　　　Enable us to live as Jesus lived,
　　　　　in steadfast opposition to sin
　　　　　and in courageous faith in the power of God.
　　　As Jesus faced the hatred of enemies
　　　　　　and the desertion of friends on earth,
　　　　　so may we be prepared to face manfully
　　　　　　and with unfailing faith
　　　　　whatever opposition or enmity
　　　　　our service of Christ may arouse against us,
　　　in certain hope that in all things
　　　　　we can be strengthened through him
　　　　　　who has overcome the world.

235.　GOD, who didst allow the swords and staves of
　　　　　　　　　　　armed men
　　　　to oppose the pure majesty of the Prince of peace:
　　　　　　　Grant us, his disciples,
　　　　　　　to fear no threatenings of force
　　　　　　　　nor assaults of evil,
　　　　but to stand immovable in the might of thy Spirit
　　　　　　　and the testimony of faith;
　　　　　through the same Jesus Christ our Lord.

236.　WE ADORE THEE, O CHRIST,
　　　　and we bless thy holy Name
　　　in all thy holy Churches that are in all the world,
　　　　because by thy holy Cross
　　　　thou hast redeemed the world.　*Amen.*

58. If the world hate you

Christ's prayer for his followers in times of opposition

I do not pray that thou shouldst take them out of the
world, but that thou shouldst keep them from the evil
one.

S. John 17: 15

Christ's followers must expect the treatment that he received

Remember the word that I said to you, A servant is not
greater than his master. If they persecuted me, they
will persecute you; if they kept my word,
they will keep yours also.

S. John 15: 20

Opposition brings with it opportunities for witness

I want you to know, brethren, that what has happened
to me has really served to advance the gospel, so that
it has become known throughout the whole praetorian
guard and to all the rest that my imprisonment is for
Christ; and most of the brethren have been made
confident in the Lord because of my imprisonment,
and are much more bold to speak the word of God
without fear.

Philippians 1: 12-14

Let us pray:

for our brethren enduring opposition for their faith today,
that they may see opportunities for witness in every
difficulty;
that hope and courage may be strengthened by the
knowledge that the whole Church is praying for them;
that we ourselves may not shrink from unpopularity,
ridicule and opposition for the sake of our Lord, nor
fail in love towards those who oppose us.

237. Lord Jesus Christ, we pray thee for our fellow-Christians in all parts of the world who are facing difficulties, and who are tempted to turn back because their way is hard. Make them brave and steadfast, and may their loyal witness draw others to thee; for thy Name's sake.

Let us pray with a Chinese Christian
238. O Lord, we pray thee that thy Church, in the midst of tribulations and temptations, may remain steadfast and faithful to thy mission.

May thy followers, in the midst of unpopularity and persecution, be not ashamed of acknowledging thy lordship, nor of witnessing to thy gospel of salvation. O God, give them courage, hope and strength that they may be able to stand the severe tests and overcome the temptations. May they be conscious of the fact that Christ is far above all principality and power and might and dominion, and every name that is named, not only in this world, but also in that which is to come.

We pray that through all trials, thy servants may come out like Apostle Paul: troubled, yet not distressed; perplexed, but not in despair; persecuted, but not forsaken; cast down, but not destroyed.

Help them and strengthen them, O Lord. We pray in the name of Jesus Christ, our Lord and Saviour.

The Lord's Prayer

239. Blessed are ye when men shall reproach you, and persecute you, and say all manner of evil against you falsely, for my sake. Rejoice, and be exceeding glad: for great is your reward in heaven. *Amen.*

And when they had called in the apostles, they beat them
and charged them not to speak in the name of Jesus,
and let them go.

Then they left the presence of the council, rejoicing that
they were counted worthy to suffer dishonor for the name.
And every day in the temple and at home they did not
cease teaching and preaching Jesus as the Christ.

Acts 5 : 40-42

Beloved, do not be surprised at the fiery ordeal which comes
upon you to prove you, as though something strange were
happening to you. But rejoice in so far as you share
Christ's sufferings, that you may also rejoice and be glad
when his glory is revealed.

If you are reproached for the name of Christ, you are
blessed, because the spirit of glory and of God rests upon
you.

I Peter 4 : 12-14

We are afflicted in every way, but not crushed; perplexed,
but not driven to despair; persecuted, but not forsaken;
struck down, but not destroyed; always carrying in the
body the death of Jesus, so that the life of Jesus may also
be manifested in our bodies.

II Corinthians 4 : 8-10

Let us pray:
for our brethren in different parts of the world who suffer
for their faith, that they may be more than conquerors
through him who loves them;

for all who are tempted through fear or pain to com-
promise their faith or deny their Master;

for ourselves that we may never be ashamed to show that
we belong to Christ.

240. ALMIGHTY GOD, who hast shown us in the life and teaching of thy Son the true way of blessedness, thou hast also shown us in his suffering and death that the path of love may lead to the cross, and the reward of faithfulness may be a crown of thorns.

Give us grace to learn these hard lessons.

May we take up our cross and follow Christ, in the strength of patience and the constancy of faith; and see even in our darkest hour of trial and anguish the shining of the eternal light.

241. O ALMIGHTY GOD, who hast taught us that they who suffer for thee shall see of the travail of their souls and shall be satisfied, and that they who pour out their souls unto death shall divide the spoil with the strong:

We thank thee that in the cross of thy dear Son thou hast revealed the secret of spiritual victory out of utter defeat, and that the obedience of Good Friday shall lead to the triumph of Easter.

Keep this faith before the eyes of our brethren who suffer for thee and transform our prayers into courage and love for them.

242. O LORD CHRIST, who, when thine hour was come, didst go without fear among those who sought thy life: Grant us grace to confess thee before men, without arrogance and without fear, that thy holy name may be glorified.

The Lord's Prayer

243. BE IN ALL WHO SUFFER FOR THEE, O CHRIST,
    and give them thy steadfast strength,
        that as they suffer for thee,
        thou mayest be in them
    and carry them and their cross to victory and life.

60. Interceding

Our Lord's command and promise
>Ask, and it will be given you; seek and you will find;
>knock, and it will be opened to you.
>For every one who asks receives, and he who seeks finds,
>and to him who knocks it will be opened.

>If you abide in me, and my words abide in you, ask
>whatever you will, and it shall be done for you.

S. Matthew 7: 7-8. S. John 15: 7

Prayer for the Church's mission
>When he saw the crowds, he had compassion for them,
>because they were harassed and helpless, like sheep
>without a shepherd. Then he said to his disciples,
>>The harvest is plentiful, but the laborers are few;
>>pray therefore the Lord of the harvest to send out
>>laborers into his harvest.

S. Matthew 9: 36-38

A missionary's request for prayer
>Continue steadfastly in prayer, being watchful in it with
>thanksgiving; and pray for us also, that God may
>open to us a door for the word, to declare the mystery
>of Christ, on account of which I am in prison, that I
>may make it clear, as I ought to speak.

Colossians 4: 2-4

Meditation
>The best prayer of all is that God's will shall be done in
>and for those for whom we pray.
>Prayer assumes that we are trying to co-operate with
>God's will.

OUR FATHER . . .

244. LORD, HELP ME TO PRAY;
            to desire to pray,
            to delight to pray.
    Make all my supplication joyful with faith,
            joyful with hope,
            joyful with love:
    joyful with thine own Spirit interceding with me,
        urgent with his yearning behind my inattention,
        wide with his wisdom behind my dim-sightedness,
        burning with his fire behind my lukewarmth:
    joyful in the fellowship of the prayers of thy saints,
                and of thy whole Church, above, below;
    through him who in heaven maketh intercession
                continually,
            thy Son Jesus Christ our Lord.

Let us also pray with St Paul

245. O FATHER OF OUR LORD JESUS CHRIST,
    from whom every family in heaven and on earth
            is named:
    Grant that, according to the riches of thy glory,
    we may be strengthened with power through thy Spirit,
        that Christ may dwell in our hearts by faith;
        that we, being rooted and grounded in love,
        may be strong to apprehend with all the saints
    what is the length and breadth and height and depth,
    and to know the love of Christ which passeth knowledge.

246. WE PRAY THEE, O LORD OUR FATHER, for all who
    profess and call themselves Christians, that their love
    may abound yet more and more unto the day of
    Christ; that they may be sincere and void of offence,
    being filled with the fruits of righteousness which are
    through Jesus Christ unto thy praise and glory, now
    and for ever.

247. GOD FORBID that I should sin against the Lord
            in ceasing to pray for you. *Amen*

61. More blessed to give

We want you to know, brethren, about the grace of God
    which has been shown in the churches of Macedonia,
for in a severe test of affliction, their abundance of joy and
    their extreme poverty have overflowed in a wealth of
    liberality on their part. For they gave according to their
    means, as I can testify, and beyond their means, of their
    own free will . . .
but first they gave themselves to the Lord.

II Corinthians 8: 1-3, 5

He looked up and saw the rich putting their gifts into the
    treasury; and he saw a poor widow put in two copper
    coins. And he said,
        Truly I tell you, this poor widow has put in more than
        all of them; for they all contributed out of their
        abundance, but she out of her poverty put in all the
        living that she had.

S. Luke 21: 1-4

In all things I have shown you that by so toiling one must
help the weak, remembering the words of the Lord Jesus,
how he said,
    It is more blessed to give than to receive.

Acts 20: 35 (A.V.)

Let us remember:
    that the Church depends on the gifts of its faithful people
        to carry on its mission to the world
    that we do not give much to God if we only provide
        amenities for our own local church
    that our Lord accepts all we do to relieve the needs of
        others as if it were done to himself
    that our money and possessions are to be held in a spirit
        of stewardship

The Lord's Prayer

158

248. O GOD, WHO DESIREST no sacrifice,
    but a humble and contrite spirit;
who wilt accept no gifts,
    save such as come from a good and honest heart:
Save us, we pray thee, lest we come before thee
    with hands not free from stain;
and mercifully accept the offering of ourselves,
    who have nothing worthy to offer
        but what is from thee,
    and dare not offer
    what is not hallowed by thee;
        for Jesus Christ's sake.

249. O ALMIGHTY GOD, whose blessed Son though he was
        rich
        yet for our sakes did become poor,
    that we through his poverty might become rich:
Grant us the spirit of generous self-giving
    that we may further the work of thy Church
        and relieve those who are in need.
Help us who have received so freely from thee
        to give as freely in our turn,
    and so share the blessedness of giving
    as well as the happiness of receiving.
We ask this in the name of him who gave himself
        for the life of the world,
    even thy Son, Jesus Christ, our Lord.

250. THINE, O LORD, is the greatness, and the power,
    and the glory, and the victory, and the majesty:
for all that is in the heaven and in the earth is thine;
    thine is the kingdom, O Lord,
    and thou art exalted as head above all.
        All things come of thee,
    and of thine own do we give thee. *Amen.*

62. *Who will go for us?*

Then flew one of the seraphim to me, having in his hand a
burning coal which he had taken with tongs from the altar.
And he touched my mouth, and said:
  Behold, this has touched your lips; your guilt is taken
  away, and your sin forgiven.
And I heard the voice of the Lord saying,
  Whom shall I send, and who will go for us?
Then I said, Here I am! Send me.

Isaiah 6: 6-8

But how are men to call upon him in whom they have not
  believed? And how are they to believe in him of whom
  they have never heard? And how are they to hear
  without a preacher? And how can men preach unless
  they are sent? As it is written, How beautiful are the
  feet of those who preach good news!

Romans 10: 14, 15

All authority in heaven and on earth has been given to me.
  Go therefore and make disciples of all nations, baptizing
  them in the name of the Father and of the Son and of the
  Holy Spirit, teaching them to observe all that I have
  commanded you;
and lo, I am with you always, to the close of the age.

S. Matthew 28: 18-20

Let us pray:
  that Christians everywhere may realize that there is no
    participation in Christ without participation in his
    mission to the world;
  that the Church may be conscious of its calling as the
    Body of Christ to fulfil this mission;
  for the missionary societies which for many generations
    have accepted the responsibility for this work, often
    when the Church's sense of mission has been weak;

160

for mission boards and councils through which the Churches now seek to fulfil their obligation;
that Christians everywhere may offer themselves willingly in this service.

The Lord's Prayer

251. O GOD OUR FATHER, help us to realize the greatness of our calling in Christ. Fill us with fresh visions of thy love, thy power, thy wonderful purpose for thy creation; inspire and strengthen us with the sense of being called in the Body of Christ—made one with our Lord, and in Him with one another.

252. O LORD, without whom our labour is but lost,
and with whom thy little ones go forth as the mighty:
Be present to all works in thy Church
which are undertaken according to thy will;
and grant to thy labourers a pure intention,
patient faith, sufficient success upon earth,
and the bliss of serving thee in heaven;
through Jesus Christ our Lord.

253. GRANT, WE PRAY THEE, O LORD, to all who serve thee in the organization of the world mission of thy Church the vision of thy purpose for the world, a share of thy love for men, and a faith that will not be daunted by difficulty or lack of response.
Let them ever be mindful that thy kingdom is advanced not by might nor by power, but by thy Spirit.
Help them to believe that if they first seek thy kingdom and thy righteousness they shall receive sufficient grace for the doing of thy will.
We ask this in the name of Jesus Christ, our Lord.

63. Spreading the Truth

Every man needs the Christian message in his own language

> We hear them telling in their own tongues the mighty works of God. *Acts 2: 11*

The Word can be passed on from one church to another

> And when this letter has been read among you, have it read also in the church of the Laodiceans, and see that you read also the letter from Laodicea. *Colossians 4: 16*

Three-fifths of the people in the world cannot yet read

> Have you not read this scripture? . . . *S. Mark 12: 10*

> Have ye not read what was said to you by God? . . .
> *S. Matthew 22: 31*

> Do you understand what you are reading? *Acts 8: 30*

New methods of communication can help to spread the gospel

> Their voice goes out through all the earth, and their words to the end of the world. *Psalm 19: 4*

> He sends forth his command to the earth; his word runs swiftly. *Psalm: 147: 15*

Let us meditate on the power of the printed word—

> it can bring the thought of the writer to many readers;
> it can be produced in thousands of copies;
> it can link the centuries and refresh the memory;
> it can be hidden and read in secret;
> it can remain behind when people have to leave.
> But it is of no value unless people are able to read.

. . . on the modern methods of communication—

> which can bring news so quickly from one part of the world to another;
> which can speak to people in their own homes;
> which can be used to spread lies, suspicion and hatred, or truth, trust, and understanding friendship.

Let us pray:

for writers and artists
    translators and journalists
    printers and booksellers
    teachers of the illiterate
    broadcasters in television and radio
that through them the knowledge of truth, beauty, love
    and goodness may be spread throughout the world;
for all engaged in spreading the gospel of Christ, that they
    may use every available means;
for all who cannot yet read, that their fellowmen will
    help them to do so and enable them to find truth and
    that new life which is God's will for them.

The Lord's Prayer

254. DIRECT AND BLESS, WE BESEECH THEE, LORD, those
      who in this our generation speak where many
      listen, and write what many read; that they may
      do their part in making the heart of the people
      wise, its mind sound, and its will righteous; to the
      honour of Jesus Christ our Lord.

255. O ALMIGHTY GOD, WE THANK THEE
      for the wonderful universe thou hast created
        and for its secrets revealed to men.
    We thank thee that men may speak to one another
      across the centuries and across the continents,
        annihilating space and time.
    Grant that all means of communication may be used
      for the purpose of truth, peace and love,
        so that all men may hear the good news of the gospel
      and find their brotherhood in thee,
    through Jesus Christ, thine own Eternal Word.

256. BLESSING, and glory and wisdom, and thanksgiving,
      and honour, and power, and might,
        be unto our God for ever and ever. *Amen.*

X. LAST THINGS

64. The Lord from Heaven

But the day of the Lord will come like a thief,
    and then the heavens will pass away with a loud noise,
    and the elements will be dissolved with fire,
    and the earth and the works that are upon it
           will be burned up.
Since all these things are thus to be dissolved,
     what sort of persons ought you to be
     in lives of holiness and godliness,
    waiting for and hastening the coming
          of the day of God? . . .
But according to his promise we wait for new heavens
    and a new earth in which righteousness dwells.

II Peter 3: 10-12, 13

Then comes the end,
    when he delivers the kingdom to God the Father
         after destroying every rule
         and every authority and power.
For he must reign
    until he has put all his enemies under his feet.
    The last enemy to be destroyed is death. . . .
When all things are subjected to him,
    then the Son himself will also be subjected
      to him who put all things under him,
    that God may be everything to every one.

I Corinthians 15: 24-26, 28

And this gospel of the kingdom will be preached
     throughout the whole world,
  as a testimony to all nations;
and then the end will come.

S. Matthew 24: 14

Let us remember:
  that one day our Lord will return in majesty and
    judgement;
  that only the Father knows the time of the end;
  that we are living in the last days, the age between our
    Lord's first and second comings.

Let us pray:
  that we may so live that when our Lord comes he may
    find us faithful, watchful, expectant;
  that by preaching the gospel to all nations we may hasten
    the time of his coming;
  that as we came from God, we may go to God and ever
    belong to God.

257. MAKE US, WE BESEECH THEE, O LORD,
     watchful and heedful in awaiting the coming
       of thy Son Christ our Lord;
  that when he shall stand at the door and knock,
      he may find us,
    not sleeping in carelessness and sin,
     but awake and rejoicing in his praises;
  through the same Jesus Christ our Lord.

258. WITHHOLD NOT FROM ME, O MY GOD,
     the best, the Spirit of thy dear Son:
    that in that Day when the judgement is set
    I may be presented unto thee
     not blameless, but forgiven,
     not effectual but faithful,

not holy but persevering,
 without desert but accepted,
because he hath pleaded the causes of my soul,
 and redeemed my life.

259. O SAVIOUR CHRIST, we pray thee
  for the millions who have never heard thy name
   or known thy love.
  Make thyself known to them
   in whatever state they be,
   in this world or the next.
  Help us to proclaim thy gospel
   in urgency and love,
  that men may not be left
   to live without thee
   or die without thee,
  but may know with us the joy
   of sin forgiven,
   of overflowing grace,
   of peace in life and death,
  and of good things prepared
   for them that love thee.
 O Saviour of the world, fetch them home
  that they may be saved for ever.

The Lord's Prayer

260. THE GOD OF PEACE himself sanctify you wholly;
  and may your spirit and soul and body
   be preserved entire,
    without blame
  at the coming of our Lord Jesus Christ. *Amen.*

65. Where Judgement Begins

Our Lord's presence always brings judgement

Behold, I send my messenger to prepare the way before me, and the Lord whom you seek will suddenly come to his temple; the messenger of the covenant in whom you delight, behold, he is coming, says the Lord of hosts.

But who can endure the day of his coming, and who can stand when he appears?

For he is like a refiner's fire and like fullers' soap; he will sit as a refiner and purifier of silver, and he will purify the sons of Levi and refine them like gold and silver, till they present right offerings to the Lord.

Malachi 3: 1-3

A warning from Israel's rejection

But if some of the branches were broken off, and you, a wild olive shoot, were grafted in their place to share the richness of the olive tree, do not boast over the branches. If you do boast, remember it is not you that support the root, but the root that supports you.

You will say, Branches were broken off so that I might be grafted in.

That is true. They were broken off because of their unbelief, but you stand fast only through faith.

So do not become proud, but stand in awe. For if God did not spare the natural branches, neither will he spare you.

Romans 11: 17-21

The need for repentance

But I have this against you, that you have abandoned the love you had at first.

Remember then from what you have fallen, repent and do the works you did at first. If not, I will come to you and remove your lampstand from its place, unless you repent. . . .

He who has an ear, let him hear what the Spirit says to the churches.

To him who conquers I will grant to eat of the tree of life, which is in the paradise of God.

Revelation 2: 4, 5, 7

O Lord, forgive:
> our failure to see in Jesus Christ the Lord of all good life, and the Saviour of all mankind,
>
> *O Lord, forgive*
>
> our coldness and lack of zeal for the Kingdom of God,
> our past unfaithfulness to Christ's commission to his Church,
> our tendency to put loyalty to our country before loyalty to the Church,
> our temptations to compromise with the world and to acquiesce in situations which we know to be wrong,
> our frequent failures to champion social justice and to be the hope of depressed and suffering peoples,
> our failure to lay to heart the divisions of Christ's Body,
> our small sacrifices, our neglected opportunities, our forgetfulness of those who rely on our prayers.
>
> *O Lord, forgive.*

261. O Lord, WE BESEECH THEE, let thy continual pity cleanse and defend thy Church; and, because it cannot continue in safety without thy succour, preserve it evermore by thy help and goodness; through Jesus Christ our Lord.

262. O MOST MERCIFUL FATHER,
> we confess that we have done little
> to forward thy kingdom in the world,
> and to advance thy glory.
> We would humble ourselves before thee
> for our past neglects,
> and seek for thy forgiveness.
> Pardon our shortcomings.

168

Give us greater zeal for thy glory.
Make us more ready and more diligent
   by our prayers, by our alms,
      and by our lives,
   to spread abroad the knowledge of thy truth,
   and to enlarge the boundaries of thy kingdom.
May the love of Christ constrain us,
and the power of the Holy Spirit renew us,
   that we may serve thee more worthily
      in the days to come;
      through Jesus Christ our Lord.

The Lord's Prayer

263. THE GOD OF PATIENCE and of comfort
      grant you to be of the same mind
         one with another
         according to Christ Jesus:
            that with one accord
         ye may with one mouth glorify
      the God and Father of our Lord Jesus Christ. *Amen.*

66. *Sir, we would see Jesus*

Now there were certain Greeks among those that went up
to worship at the feast; these therefore came to Philip,
which was of Bethsaida of Galilee, and asked him, saying,
Sir, we would see Jesus.

S. John 12: 20-21 (R.V.)

Now when they saw the boldness of Peter and John, and
perceived that they were uneducated, common men, they
wondered; and they recognized that they had been with
Jesus.

Acts 4:

Have this mind among yourselves, which you have in
    Christ Jesus,
who, though he was in the form of God, did not count
    equality with God a thing to be grasped, but emptied
    himself, taking the form of a servant, being born in the
    likeness of men.
And being found in human form he humbled himself and
    became obedient unto death, even death on a cross.

Philippians 2: 5-8

Let us reflect:

on the world's demand that it shall see Jesus
    in the life of his Church
    and in the lives of individual Christians.
From every part of the world comes abundant testimony
    that the more Christians have conformed to the spirit
    of Christ the more have people been drawn to
    Christianity and Christ.
It is in the lives of ordinary Christians,
    more even than in the gospel records
    or in the official teaching of the Church,
that non-Christians will judge Christianity
    and our Lord himself.

264. O Christ, whose wondrous birth meaneth nothing
        unless we be born again,
    whose death and sacrifice nothing
        unless we die unto sin,
    whose resurrection nothing if thou be risen alone:
    Raise and exalt us, O Saviour,
        both now to the estate of grace
        and hereafter to the state of glory;
    where with the Father and the Holy Spirit
        thou livest and reignest,
            God for ever and ever.

265. O God, the God of all goodness and of all grace,
        who art worthy of a greater love
        than we can either give or understand:
    Fill our hearts, we beseech thee,
        with such love toward thee
        that nothing may seem too hard for us to do
                or to suffer
            in obedience to thy will;
    and grant that thus loving thee,
        we may become daily more like unto thee,
    and finally obtain the crown of life
    which thou hast promised to those that love thee;
        through Jesus Christ our Lord.

Prayer of a Chinese woman after learning to read
266. We are going home to many who cannot read.
        So, Lord, make us to be Bibles
    so that those who cannot read the Book
            can read it in us.

The Lord's Prayer

267. Whatsoever we do, in word or in deed,
    may we do all in the name of the Lord Jesus,
    giving thanks to God the Father through him.

67. Ever Interceding

Our Lord's prayer for a tempted disciple
> Simon, Simon, behold, Satan demanded to have you,
> that he might sift you like wheat, but I have prayed
> for you that your faith may not fail; and when you have
> turned again, strengthen your brethren.

S. Luke 22: 31, 32

His prayer for all his disciples
> Holy Father, keep them in thy name which thou hast
> given me, that they may be one, even as we are one. . . .
> I in them and thou in me, that they may become
> perfectly one,
> so that the world may know that thou hast sent me and
> hast loved them even as thou hast loved me. . . .
> I do not pray that thou shouldst take them out of the
> world, but that thou shouldst keep them from the
> evil one.

S. John 17: 11, 23, 15

His constant intercession in heaven
> For we have not a high priest who is unable to sympathize
> with our weaknesses, but one who in every respect has
> been tempted as we are, yet without sinning. . . .
> For Christ has entered, not into a sanctuary made with
> hands, a copy of the true one, but into heaven itself,
> now to appear in the presence of God on our behalf. . . .
> Consequently he is able for all time to save those who
> draw near to God through him, since he always lives
> to make intercession for them.

Hebrews 4: 15; 9: 24; 7: 25

Let us in silence lift our hearts to heaven,
> to the presence of Christ, our great High Priest,
who is ever interceding for us.

The Lord's Prayer

268. ALMIGHTY AND ETERNAL GOD, whose worship brake forth from the ancient sanctuary at the rending of the veil, to become the salvation and joy of the whole earth:

Lead us now and ever into the Holiest by the new and living way which thou hast dedicated for us in thy Son, incarnate and crucified, our everlasting Lord: to whom with thee and the Holy Spirit, be all honour and dominion, world without end.

269. O LORD JESUS CHRIST, who hast left us for a while, giving us the promise that thou wilt come again, and receive us to abide with thee for ever:

Grant us such communion with thyself
    that our souls may be continually athirst
    for that time when we shall behold thee in thy
        glory;
who livest and reignest with the Father
and the Holy Spirit, one God, world without end.

270. O LORD, WE THANK THEE for the redeeming power
        of the unceasing intercession
    and for the stream of love which is ever flowing
        from thy throne of grace.
    Help us to remember thy prayers for us
        in our time of temptation or need.
Help us to pray with thee for the needs of all men,
        lifting them into thy presence
    so that thy grace may meet their every need.
For thou art the Lover and Saviour of all.

271. NOW UNTO HIM that is able to keep you from falling,
        and to present you faultless
before the presence of his glory with exceeding joy;
        to the only wise God our Saviour,
    be glory and majesty, dominion and power,
            both now and ever. *Amen.*

68. According to your faith

According to your faith be it done to you.

If you have faith as a grain of mustard seed, you will say to this mountain, Move hence to yonder place, and it will move; and nothing will be impossible to you.

S. Matthew 9: 29; 17: 20

With men it is impossible, but not with God;
  for all things are possible with God.
All things are possible to him who believes.

S. Mark 10: 27; 9: 23

This is the victory that overcomes the world, our faith.

I John 5: 4

Now faith is the assurance of things hoped for, the conviction of things not seen. . . .
For Moses endured as seeing him who is invisible.

Hebrews 11: 1, 27

For I know whom I have believed. *II Timothy 1: 12*

Let us pray

272. LORD, WE BELIEVE IN THEE, help thou our unbelief;
    we love thee, yet not with perfect hearts as we would;
    we long for thee, yet not with our full strength;
    we trust in thee, yet not with our whole mind.
      Accept our faith, our love,
        our longing to know and serve thee,
        our trust in thy power to keep us.
      What is cold do thou kindle,
      what is lacking do thou supply;
      through Jesus Christ our Lord.

273. O LORD OUR GOD, in whose hands is the issue of all
things, who requirest from thy stewards not
success, but faithfulness:
Give us such faith in thee, and in thy sure purpose
that we measure not our lives by what we have
done, or failed to do, but by our obedience to thy
will.

274. O THOU WHO ART HEROIC LOVE, keep alive in our
hearts that adventurous spirit which makes men
scorn the way of safety, so that thy will be done.
For so only shall we be worthy of those courageous
souls who in every age have ventured all in
obedience to thy call, and for whom the trumpets
have sounded on the other side; through Jesus
Christ our Lord.

The Lord's Prayer

275. LORD, INCREASE MY FAITH,
that I may embrace everything that is thy will.
Lord, increase my faith
that the mountains of difficulty may be removed.
Lord, increase my faith that I may never be
at a loss for some creative action for thee.
Lord, increase my faith that I may never be
impatient or frustrated.
Lord, increase my faith that I may run to thee
in every situation.
Lord, increase my faith that I may trust thee
in seeming failure or defeat.
Lord, increase my faith that I may endure
as seeing thee who art visible only to the eye of
faith.
Lord, fill me with faith, hope and love,
this day and always.

69. *Jesus Only*

After this many of his disciples drew back and no longer
went about with him.

Jesus said to the twelve, Will you also go away?

Simon Peter answered him, Lord, to whom shall we go?
You have the words of eternal life; and we have believed,
and have come to know, that you are the Holy One of
God.

S. John 6: 66-69

But whatever gain I had, I counted as loss for the sake of
Christ. Indeed I count everything as loss because of the
surpassing worth of knowing Christ Jesus my Lord.

For his sake I have suffered the loss of all things, and count
them as refuse, in order that I may gain Christ . . . that
I may know him and the power of his resurrection, and
may share his sufferings, becoming like him in his death.

Philippians 3: 7, 8, 10

I have been crucified with Christ; it is no longer I who live,
but Christ who lives in me; and the life I now live in the
flesh I live by faith in the Son of God, who loved me and
gave himself for me.

Galatians 2: 20

Jesus Christ is the same yesterday and today and for ever.

Hebrews 13: 8

His servants shall worship him; . . . they shall see his face.

Revelation 22: 3, 4

Acts of Desire

276. LIKE AS THE HART desireth the water-brooks, so
longeth my soul after thee, O God.

My soul is athirst for God, yea, even for the living
God; when shall I come to appear before the
presence of God?

277. O GOD, THOU ART MY GOD, early will I seek thee.
My soul thirsteth for thee, my flesh also longeth after
thee in a barren and dry land where no water is.
Thus have I looked for thee in holiness that I might
behold thy power and glory.

Acts of Trust

278. THE LORD IS MY LIGHT, and my salvation; whom
then shall I fear? The Lord is the strength of my
life; of whom then shall I be afraid?

279. I KNOW whom I have believed, and I am persuaded
that he is able to guard that which I have committed unto him against that day.

Acts of Love

280. I WILL LOVE THEE, O LORD my strength; the Lord is
my stony rock, and my defence, my Saviour, my
God, and my might, in whom I will trust,
my buckler, the horn also of my salvation, and
my refuge.

281. LORD, THOU KNOWEST all things; thou knowest that
I love thee.

The Promises

282. All the ends of the earth shall remember and turn to
the Lord; and all the families of the nations shall
worship before him.

283. By myself I have sworn, from my mouth has gone
forth in righteousness, a word that shall not return:
To me every knee shall bow, every tongue shall
swear.

284. All things are yours . . . the world, or life, or death,
or things present, or things to come; all are
yours;
and ye are Christ's; and Christ is God's.

70. Come and Worship

God is spirit, and those who worship him must worship in
spirit and truth. . . .
for such the Father seeks to worship him.

S. John 4: 24, 23

Worship the Lord in holy array; tremble before him, all
the earth! Say among the nations,
> The Lord reigns! Yea, the world is established, it
> shall never be moved; he will judge the peoples with
> equity.

Psalm 96: 9, 10

Great and wonderful are thy deeds, O Lord God the
Almighty!
Just and true are thy ways, O King of the ages!
Who shall not fear and glorify thy name, O Lord?
For thou alone art holy.
All nations shall come and worship thee,
for thy judgements have been revealed.

Revelation 15: 3, 4

Let us remember:
the saints, martyrs and angels before God's throne,
unceasing in their worship
before the unclouded vision of God;
the Holy Church throughout the world,
never silent in the worship of God;
the primary duty of men—to worship God the Creator.

Let us pray:
for a deepening sense of worship as we behold the
unfolding wonder of the universe;
for hearts full of praise as we understand more clearly
God's great purpose of love for the world;
for Christians of all nations, that in the common faith
they may express their worship in differing ways, native
to their own heritage;

that as Churches come together in unity, their worship may be deepened and enriched by the contribution which each one brings.

The Lord's Prayer

285. O THE DEPTH OF THE RICHES both of the wisdom and knowledge of God! how unsearchable are his judgements, and his ways past finding out!
For who hath known the mind of the Lord? or who hath been his counsellor? Or who hath first given to him, and it shall be recompensed unto him again?
For of him, and through him, and to him, are all things: to whom be glory for ever.

286. ALMIGHTY GOD, unto whom all hearts be open, all desires known, and from whom no secrets are hid:
Cleanse the thoughts of our hearts by the inspiration of thy Holy Spirit, that we may perfectly love thee, and worthily magnify thy holy Name;
through Christ our Lord.

287. GRANT TO ME, O LORD, to worship thee
            in spirit and in truth;
          to submit all my nature to thee,
that my conscience may be quickened by thy holiness,
          my mind nourished by thy truth,
          my imagination purified by thy beauty.
Help me to open my heart to thy love
and to surrender my will to thy purpose.
          So may I lift up my heart to thee
          in selfless adoration and love.
          Through Jesus Christ my Lord.

288. O PRAISE GOD IN HIS HOLINESS;
          praise him according to his excellent greatness . . .
Let everything that hath breath praise the Lord.

COMMITMENT TO JESUS CHRIST

289. JESUS CHRIST, I want you:
        for my own sake,
        for your sake,
        for the sake of others.

      I want you for my own sake:
        because I am nothing,
        because I am so weak,
        because I am a sinner.

      I want you for your sake:
        that I may know you,
        that I may love you,
        that I may become like you.

      I want you for the sake of others:
        that I may do them no harm,
        that I may do them only good,
        that I may give you to them.

  JESUS CHRIST, you want me:
        for my sake,
        for your own sake,
        for the sake of others.

      You want me for my sake:
        because you made me,
        because you died for me,
        because you have chosen me.

You want me for your own sake:
    that your joy may be in me,
    that where you are I also may be,
    that you may live in me.

You want me for the sake of others:
    that through me you may heal them,
    that through me you may teach them,
    that through me you may live in them.

THEN, JESUS CHRIST,
    take as your right
    receive as my gift
    all my liberty
        my memory, my understanding, my will
        all that I have
        all that I am
        all that I can be
Thou hast given it all to me
    to thee, O Lord, I restore it
All is thine
    dispose of it according to thy will.

Give me thy love
Give me thy grace
    and I am rich enough.
Nor ask I anything beside.

A NOTE ON SOURCES

1. Revelation 4: 11 R.V.
2. Hebrews 1: 10-12 R.V.
3. Wisdom 11: 24-26
4. Liturgy of St. James. *Prayers New and Old*, A. W. Robinson (Student Christian Movement Press)
5. *Daily Prayer*, Compiled by Eric Milner-White & G. W. Briggs (Oxford University Press)
6. Nestorian Liturgy, *Daily Prayer*
7. Luke 1: 68-69
8. *Book of Common Prayer* (*B.C.P.*)
9. *New Every Morning* (British Broadcasting Corporation)
10. *Daily Prayer*
11. *A Devotional Diary*, arr. J. H. Oldham (S.C.M. Press)
12. Based on *Brihadaranyaka Upanishad* I: 3, 27, before 600 B.C.
13. *B.C.P.* as proposed 1928
14. Eric Fenn. *New Every Morning*
15. *After the Third Collect*, ed. E. Milner-White (Mowbray)
16. *Per Christum Vinces*, Compiled by E. M. Barton (Longmans, Green)
17. *Daily Prayer*
18. The Compiler
19. Romans 15: 13 R.V.
20. *Prayers of the World-Wide Church*, (Society for the Propagation of the Gospel)
21. Te Deum Laudamus
22. Eric Fenn. *New Every Morning*
23. The Compiler
24. The Compiler
25. Bishop Andrewes
26. Bishop of Southwell (adapted) in *The Kingdom, the Power and the Glory*, E. Milner-White (O.U.P.)
27. Psalm 145: 10-13
28. *Christian News-Letter*
29. Revelation 5: 13 R.S.V.
30. *Prayers of the World-Wide Church.*
31. Church Missions to Jews (adapted)
32. *B.C.P.*
33. The Compiler
34. Psalm 72: 18, 19
35. *After the Third Collect*
36. *Prayers New and Old*
37. *The Church in Germany in Prayer*, trs. Walter Kagerah and Robert A. S. Martineau (Mowbray)
38. *B.C.P.*
39. *See* Revelation 14
40. *A War Primer* (S.P.C.K.)
41. *The World at One in Prayer*, ed. Daniel Johnson Fleming (Harper Bros.)
42. *Christian News-Letter*
43. *The Life that is Light*, Archbishop Goodier, adapted (Burns Oates & Washbourne)
44. Freely adapted from Jeremy Taylor. *Daily Prayer*

45. *Meditations and Prayers*, Evelyn Underhill (Longmans, Green)
46. Archbishop William Temple
47. *With Christ in God*, S. C. Hughson (S.P.C.K. and Holy Cross Press, New York)
48. *B.C.P.*
49. *A War Primer*
50. *World Dominion XII* (1934), (World Dominion Press)
51. Mozarabic, trs. W. Bright. *Daily Prayer*
52. Erasmus
53. Christian Prayers, 1578. *Daily Prayer*
54. *The World at One in Prayer*
55. *A War Primer*
56. Collect for Easter Day, *B.C.P.*
57. Eric Fenn. *New Every Morning*
58. Source untraced
59. Bishop Cotton
60. The Compiler
61. Bishop Palmer. *Prayers of the World-Wide Church*
62. The Compiler
63. Methodist Covenant Service. *The Book of Offices* (Epworth Press)
64. St. Augustine, (354-430)
65. *B.C.P.*
66. Bishop Westcott
67. Dr. E. B. Pusey, (1800-1882)
68. Jeremy Taylor, *Jubilee of a Penitent Soul*
69. *B.C.P.*
70. Dean Vaughan. *Daily Prayer*
71. Jeremy Taylor, adapted. *After the Third Collect*
72. Dean Vaughan. *Daily Prayer*
73. *My God My Glory*, E. Milner-White (S.P.C.K.)
74. *New Every Morning*
75. St. Gregory, (540-604)
76. *New Every Morning*
77. Hebrews 13: 20-21 A.V.
78. Te Deum Laudamus
79. *B.C.P.*
80. Mozarabic Liturgy
81. The Compiler
82. Revelation 5: 13 R.V.

83. *The Book of Common Order* (of the Church of Scotland) O.U.P.
84. *B.C.P.*
85. The Compiler
86. Tenth Century
87. *A Procession of Passion Prayers*, E. Milner-White (S.P.C.K.)
88. Liturgy of St. Mark
89. *Daily Prayer*
90. *The Book of Common Order* (of the Church of Scotland)
91. *The Life that is Light* (adapted)
92. *B.C.P.*
93. *The Life that is Light* (adapted)
94. Psalm 103: 1-4
95. Luke 1: 68, 77-79
96. *B.C.P.* 1928
97. *Prayers of the World-Wide Church*
98. *Ancient Collects*, trs. W. Bright
99. S.P.G. (adapted)
100. II Corinthians 1: 3-4
101. *A Book of Prayers for Schools* (S.C.M. Press) adapted
102. *Prayers of the World-Wide Church*
103. Thomas à Kempis
104. *The Kingdom, the Power and the Glory*
105. *The Kingdom, the Power and the Glory*
106. *A Book of Prayers for Schools*
107. See Psalm 104: 14, 15
108. Bishop Paget. *Daily Prayer*
109. Frederick B. Macnutt. *The Prayer Manual* (Mowbray)
110. St. Francis of Assisi. *Daily Prayer*
111. Hebrews 13: 20-21 A.V.
112. *A Pocketful of Prayers* (Toc H)
113. *Prayers of Citizenship*, K. T. Henderson (Longmans, Green)
114. *Prayers for use in an Indian College*, J. S. Hoyland (S.P.C.K.)
115. J. H. Jowett (adapted). *A Chain of Prayer Across the Ages* (Murray)

184

116. *Daily Prayer*
117. Gelasian Sacramentary, *Ancient Collects*
118. Ephesians 3: 20-21 A.V.
119. Coronation Service, 1953
120. *B.C.P.*
121. George Adam Smith
122. Preface to Geneva Bible, attributed to King Edward VI (1537-53). *Daily Prayer*
123. Romans 15: 13 R.V.
124. *Daily Prayer*
125. *B.C.P.*
126. *New Every Morning*
127. *Daily Prayer*
128. *B.C.P.*
129. *Daily Prayer*
130. Mohammed d. A.D. 632
131. Based on Ephesians 3: 17-19
132. *After the Third Collect*
133. Dean Vaughan. *Daily Prayer*
134. *Prayers for Common Use* (U.M.C.A.)
135. *See* Psalm 67
136. *Jerusalem Chamber Fellowship of Prayer*
137. *A Procession of Passion Prayers*
138. Roman Missal. *Daily Prayer*
139. Ephesians 3: 20-21 R.V.
140. The Compiler
141. *New Every Morning*
142. *My God My Glory*
143. Romans 16: 25-27
144. *New Every Morning*
145. *B.C.P.*
146. *Daily Prayer*
147. Liturgy of St. Mark, trs. W. Bright (adapted)
148. The Compiler
149. Gothic Missal, A.D. 1680.
150. *Acts of Devotion* (S.P.C.K.)
151. *Prayers in Use at Uppingham School*, R. H. Owen (O.U.P.)
152. I Peter 5: 10-11 A.V.
153. *A Book of Prayers for Schools*
154. Collect for All Saints' Day, *B.C.P.*
155. The Compiler
156. Revelation 15: 3
157. *B.C.P.*
158. *Prayers of the World-Wide Church*
159. *The Book of Offices* (Methodist Church)
160. Revelation 1: 5-6
161. *B.C.P.*
162. *New Every Morning*
163. *The Splendour of God* (Longmans, Green)
164. Oxford Mission to Calcutta (adapted)
165. Based on I Thessalonians 5
166. W. O. Fitch
167. Psalm 84: 4-7
168. W. O. Fitch
169. Psalm 22: 22-27
170. W. O. Fitch
171. Psalm 63: 1-4
172. *B.C.P.*
173. *Prayers of the World-Wide Church*
174. R. M. Benson, S.S.J.E.
175. *Cuddesdon Office Book*
176. Ignatius Loyola (1491-1556)
177. Psalm 23
178. *B.C.P.*
179. *New Every Morning*
180. Source untraced
181. Sarum Breviary
182. *A Book of Prayers for Schools*
183. Industrial Christian Fellowship (adapted)
184. Rabindranath Tagore
185. J.R.G. Ragg in *The Church in Germany in Prayer*
186. *A Treasury of Prayers for use in Toc H* (Toc H)
187. Source untraced
188. Quoted in *Prayers in Time of War* (S.C.M. Press)
189. Source unknown
190. The Compiler
191. Psalm 22: 27-28
192. *After the Third Collect*
193. *New Every Morning*
194. *The Kingdom, the Power and the Glory*
195. Harold Anson. *New Every Morning*
196. *See* Ephesians 3: 14-15
197. *New Every Morning*
198. The Compiler
199. *New Every Morning*
200. The Compiler

201. Dean Vaughan. *Daily Prayer*
202. *After the Third Collect*
203. *Daily Prayer*
204. Philippians 4: 7
205. Gregorian Sacramentary, A.D. 590
206. The Compiler
207. Bishop Pakenham-Walsh. *Prayers New and Old*
208. Psalm 67
209. Gallican Sacramentary (Fourth Century)
210. Augustine Ralla Ram. *The World at One in Prayer*
211. Akira Ebisawa. *The World at One in Prayer*
212. *The Chinese Recorder*
213. *African Ideas of God*, Edwin W. Smith (Edinburgh House Press)
214. G. B. Molefe. *The World at One in Prayer*
215. The Compiler
216. W. A. Visser 't Hooft. *The World at One in Prayer*
217. Archbishop Laud (1573-1645). *Daily Prayer*
218. Prayer of the German Confessional Church in *The World at One in Prayer*
219. Gelasian Sacramentary
220. Harry Emerson Fosdick. *The World at One in Prayer*
221. *The World at One in Prayer*
222. *The Holy Tryst* (Church of Scotland)
223. John Ar-la-gi-ak. *The World at One in Prayer*
224. The Compiler
225. *The Kingdom, the Power and the Glory*
226. *Acts of Devotion*
227. Archbishop A. W. Averell. *The World at One in Prayer*
228. *The World at One in Prayer*
229. John Mackenzie. *The World at One in Prayer*
230. Psalm 72: 18-19
231. *B.C.P.*
232. *Acts of Devotion*
233. Leonine Sacramentary. trs. Dean Armitage Robinson
234. *A Book of Prayers for Schools*
235. *A Procession of Passion Prayers*
236. Little Brothers of St. Francis
237. The Compiler
238. S. C. Leung at Willingen, Germany, 1952
239. Matthew 5: 11, 12 R.V.
240. *A Devotional Diary*
241. The Compiler
242. *A Devotional Diary*
243. The Compiler
244. *My God My Glory*
245. Based on Ephesians 3: 14-19
246. Based on Philippians 1: 9-11
247. I Samuel 12: 23
248. *Daily Prayer*
249. The Compiler
250. I Chronicles 29: 11, 14
251. Oxford Mission to Calcutta
252. *Ancient Collects*. W. Bright
253. The Compiler
254. *The Book of Common Order* (of the Church of Scotland)
255. The Compiler
256. Revelation 7: 12
257. Gelasian. *Daily Prayer*
258. *My God My Glory*
259. The Compiler
260. I Thess. 5: 23 R.V.
261. *B.C.P.*
262. Church Missionary Society
263. Romans 15: 5-6 R.V.
264. *Cambridge Bede Book*, E. Milner-White (Longmans, Green)
265. Bishop Westcott
266. *The World at One in Prayer*
267. Colossians 3: 17
268. *A Procession of Passion Prayers*
269. *The Book of Common Order* (of the Church of Scotland)
270. The Compiler
271. Jude 24-25 A.V.
272. *A Book of Prayers for Schools*
273. *Daily Prayer*
274. *The Kingdom, the Power and the Glory*
275. The Compiler
276. Psalm 42: 1, 2
277. Psalm 63: 1-3
278. Psalm 27: 1
279. II Timothy 1: 12 R.V.

280. Psalm 18: 1
281. St. John 21: 17 R.V.
282. Psalm 22: 27 R.S.V.
283. Isaiah 45: 23 R.S.V.
284. I Corinthians 3: 21-23
285. Romans 11: 33-36
286. *B.C.P.*
287. Based on words of Arch-bishop Temple
288. Psalm 150: 1, 2, 6
289. Archbishop Goodier in *The Life that is Light* (adapted)

INDEX OF SUBJECTS

Those requiring prayers on special subjects will find considerable help in studying the table of contents on p. x-xii. More detailed information may be found in this index. The numbers given are those prefixed to the prayers; for the unnumbered Biddings, Thanksgivings and Meditations page references are included.

DATE DUE

OC 10 '78			
GAYLORD			PRINTED IN U.S.A.